35-

(40893)

BROTHERS 'TIL DEATH

BROTHERS 'TIL DEATH

*The Civil War Letters of William,
Thomas, and Maggie Jones,
1861-1865*

Irish Soldiers in the
48th New York Volunteer Regiment

Edited by
Richard M. Trimble

Mercer University Press
2000

ISBN 0-86554-698-3
MUP/H517

© 2000 Richard M. Trimble
Mercer University Press
6316 Peake Road
Macon, Georgia 31210-3960

First Edition.

CIP data are available from the Library of Congress

TABLE OF CONTENTS

To Jill,
who really showed us The South

ACKNOWLEDGMENTS

There are many people to be recognized for their contributions to this volume, but none stands out more distinctly than Robert Clark for his initial preservation and partial deciphering of the letters. A vote of thanks also goes to the LoCascio family for their steering the present editor in the direction of Mr. Clark and his remarkable letters.

Then there are the students who did the laborious work of reading, transcribing and type-scripting each letter. They were all students of mine at Manasquan High School and at Brookdale Community College:

Kim Baubles, Paul Beavis, Heather Brown, Ryan Butler, Lorissa Cheli, Sean Coughin, Elizabeth Dinklage, Brian Farley, Elizabeth Hatfield, Norah Heinle, Bill Jewell, Kate Kennedy, Ted Kupchik, Bryan Margulies, Shannon O'Brien, Kevin O'Donnell, Rusty Palmer, Bryan Price, Jesse Schulte, Troy Shield, Jennifer Smith, Kung Yan Sung, Abe Voorhees, Elizabeth Wilson, Phil Bloete, Owen Bryne, Anthony Cameli, Darryl Clancy, Katie Crossen, Darren Davis, John, Delatusch, Karriem Ferreira, Jenifer Field, Nick Foster, Jamie Locasico, Christine Martin, Ailene McGuirk, Amy Mitchell, Meg Richens, Mike Rizzo, Jana Robinson, Ian Springer, Trevor Taylor, Jim Tichenor, Rob Zupko, Shawn Laytham, Rachel Zantarsky, Pam Sorrentino, D.J. Aanensen, Noelene Cirillo, Margo English, Mike Faulhaber, Diana Griggs-Fummey, Tom Grosse, Diane Kamenitz, Nancy Levin, William Librizzi, Tara Long, Carlos Rivera, Annalisa Rohan, Glenn Roth, Hema Tekchandani, Trisha Dent, Rob Hazel, Sarah Jones, Tara McManus, and Mike Schmid are among the transcribers.

I would also like to thank professors Judy Mangan and Fred Fraterrigo for taking the time to read the manuscript and add their valued expertise. In addition, Margaret Patterson's work on the maps was equally invaluable. Another student of mine, Ketan Purohit, later helped with some additional archival discoveries about William Jones' later life.

Another word of thanks goes to Diana Griggs-Fummey, Laura Butkus, and John Broderick who typed the initial manuscript and to James

Sverapa IV who finalized the entire volume on the appropriate software. Scott Williams helped with the indexing. Andy Long, a valued colleague and friend gave of his time and expertise in a final reading of the work. I express my gratitude to him, them all. And to Marc Jolley, my editor at Mercer University Press who responded to my many inquiries with professionalism and patient encouragement.

Most of all, thank you to my wife Jeanne who endured long visits to myriad forts and battle sites with kind, quiet, and understanding patience.

INTRODUCTION

The letters contained in this volume were, for the most part, written by two brothers, William and Thomas Jones. They were most often addressed to their younger sister Maggie, although some were written to even younger siblings, Haddie and Janey.

Thomas and William were born in Down County, Ireland in 1839 and 1843, respectively. Why and when they immigrated to America is unclear, but they may have been part of the general exodus of the late 1840s spurred by the Potato Famine. Various estimates have placed the number of Irish who came to America in search of work, land, food, and dignity as between one million and 1.5 million. Many arrived in New York and sought land and work in rural New Jersey and points beyond. Those who remained behind in the cities, as so many did, suffered the injustices of discrimination, racism, Know Nothingism, and nativism. They were denied jobs under the rubric NINA ("No Irish Need Apply") or given menial service jobs at low pay only to be rounded up by police herding them into "paddy wagons" on Saturday nights ridden with alcoholic despair. Thus, the Jones family may have been among the very lucky ones.

All three sisters were probably born in America. Maggie taught school and was perhaps born in 1846 as the third child in the family. This was Bob Clark's grandmother.[1] She later married William R. Hagerman and eventually ran a boarding home in Ocean Grove, New Jersey, a Methodist camp meeting community whose blue laws extended well past the mid-point of the 20th century. Maggie died in 1912 and the boarding home was later destroyed by fire.

During the war the brothers worked as teamsters driving wagonloads of supplies to their comrades in the 48th New York State Volunteers. This is of course when they were not involved digging breastworks, hauling logs for artillery emplacements or spending lonely nights in a distant rifle-pit on picket duty.

---

[1] Owner of the letter collection.

As for the 48th New York, it was mustered into service on August 16, 1861 at the onset of the war. According to *Historical Viewpoints* by John Gerraty, the 48th was comprised of "an unusually large number of ministers."[2] Indeed, the man who commanded it was James H. Perry, a Methodist minister, West Point graduate, and a veteran of the Texas War for Independence. The regiment would become known as "Perry's Saints," a moniker which would have been an attraction for mothers sending their sons off to war and concerned with moral character, not to mention immortality. On the other hand, the 48th NYSV may have had its share of unsavory characters too. During the planning stages of an attempt to snare a bothersome Confederate ironclad gunboat in the Carolina swamps with ropes and netting, "experts" were called upon who had some ideas about prying open metal sheeting and casing. The regimental commander asked for "every man who had experience as a cracker or safeblower to step to the front." Reportedly, the entire regiment stepped forward.[3] The farm boys from Farmingdale might have stepped forward in a display of regimental unity rather than street-smart expertise. Moreover, it is suspected that the "regiment" in question might only have been one company of recent recruits or even draftees who joined late in the war.

The 48th New York also manifested a flair for the dramatic as Bell I. Wiley's classic—*The Life of Billy Yank*—reports that Perry's Saints put on Shakespearean plays, including "Richard III" while on garrison duty at Fort Pulaski. Reportedly, the men "possessed unusual dramatic talent."[4]

Colonel Perry died of a stroke in June, 1862 and typically, the regiment, including the Jones brothers, mourned the loss of their father away from home. Perry was succeeded by William B. Barton. Later, Barton was succeeded by William B. Coan in December, 1864. Another name to be considered was the Company D commander,

---

[2] John A. Gerraty, *Historical Viewpoints*, 6th ed. (New York: HarperCollins, 1991) 329.

[3] Ibid.

[4] Bell I. Wiley, *The Life of Billy Yank: The Common Soldier of the Union* (Baton Rouge: Louisiana State University Press, 1983) 176.

Captain Daniel C. Knowles, another clergyman and former teacher of languages at a Princeton seminary. Company D was the Jones' brothers outfit and it, too, had a colorful nickname, the "Die No Mores."

As sons of Ireland, William and Thomas Jones were among the 144,000 Irish-born soldiers who fought for the Union in the Civil War. Despite their foreign birth, many of them truly believed that they were fighting to preserve their newly adopted country and birthright. Joseph G. Bilby adds the notion that many Irish soldiers, especially members of the Fenians, may have considered this war as a training ground for a future attempt to liberate their native homeland from the hated British.[5] Moreover, these Irish-American soldiers often sent collections of funds and held benefits to assist their impoverished brethren back home.[6]

While Irish immigrants may have comprised only about one percent of the American population in the 1860's, they made up as much as ten percent of the Union army. The much-storied Irish Brigade was almost exclusively so. Three New York regiments, the 63rd, 69th and the 88th, initially comprised the unit which was variously called the "Connaught Rangers," "Faugh a Ballaghs," or even " Mrs. Meagher's Own" after their colorful unit commander, Thomas Meagher.[7] Many of these soldiers were veteran warriors, having seen action under the British flag in Crimea or against the Sepoys in India. Later Irish units such as the 116th Pennsylvania and the 28th Massachusetts were added to the Irish Brigade particularly as they suffered heavy losses in such battles as the Peninsula Campaign, the Bloody Lane at Antietam, before The Wall at Fredericksburg, and at Chancellorsville. Only a shadow of their numbers remained, but July, 1863 found them in the Wheatfield and behind the stone wall facing George Pickett at Gettysburg. As part of the Army of the Potomac's 2nd Corps, they were among the fightingest units in the fightingest corps

---

[5] Joseph Bilby, *The Irish Brigade* (Conshohoken, PA: Longstreet House, 1997) 29.

[6] Ibid., 97.

[7] Harry W. Pfanz, *Gettysburg-The Second Day* (Chapel Hill, NC: University of North Carolina Press, 1987) 75.

in that army. "In its four year history, the brigade lost over 4,000 men, more than were ever in it at any one time, killed and wounded. The Irish Brigade's loss of 961 soldiers killed or mortally wounded in action was exceeded by only two other brigades in the Union army."[8]

After the war, William and Thomas Jones migrated west out to Cottonwood, Kansas, and perhaps even to California. Some of the letters from that time still survive but were not chosen for this volume. While William survived the war intact, Thomas was disabled, having lost his right arm in the ill-fated assault on Battery Wagner at the mouth of the Charleston Harbor, the same fort and charge made famous by the movie *Glory*.

Editor's note to the reader: The reader will note that letters from writers other than the Joneses have been included. Since Civil War regiments were made up of local boys who often came from the same hometown, there was a special familiarity which would be absent in other future wars. Letters were shared, passed around, and read aloud. Together they enrich any collection, hence I have taken the liberty of adding appropriately insightful letters from such friends of William, Thomas, and Maggie Jones as John D. Cottrell, John A. Woodside, John D. Fogerty, Nick Hagerman, Joseph Brown, and sister Janey Jones.

---

[8] Joseph Bilby, *The Irish Brigade*, (Conshohoken, PA: Longstreet House, 1997) ix.

The pictures on this page and the following are the members of Maggie, William, and Thomas Jones Family. Precise identification is unknown.

These photos are good
Examples of cartes de
visite.

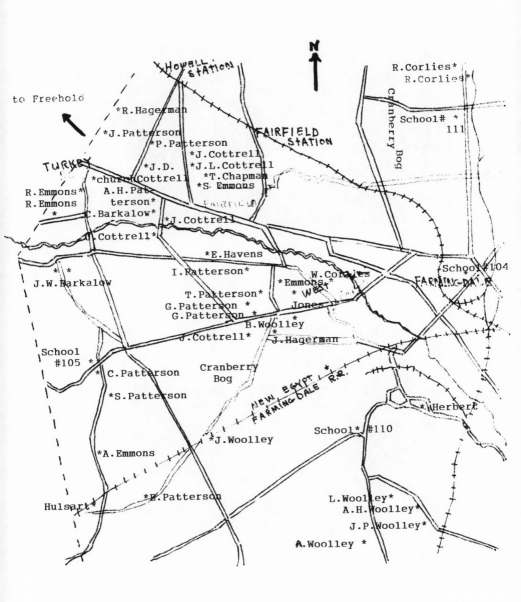

Main Sallyport Fort Pulaski, Georgia (photo by author).

Fort Pulaski's Parade Ground as it looks today. (photo by author)

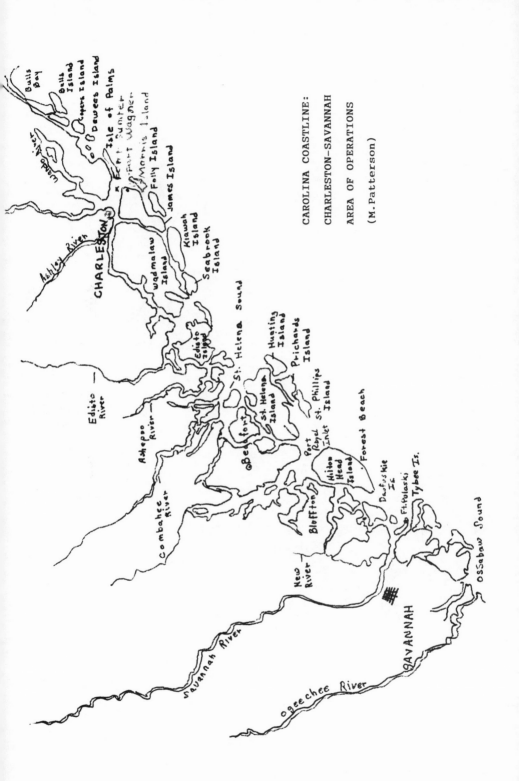

CAROLINA COASTLINE:

CHARLESTON-SAVANNAH

AREA OF OPERATIONS

(M. Patterson)

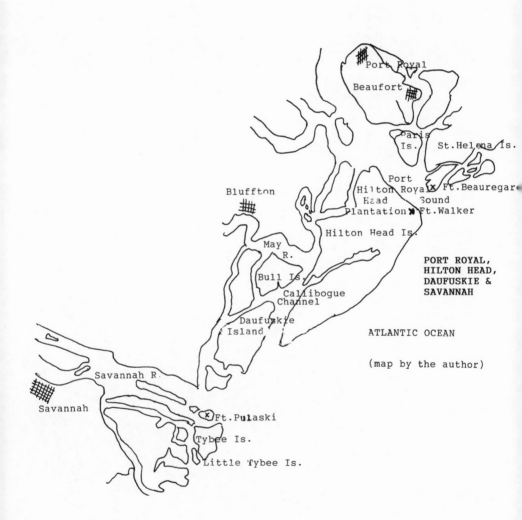

Port Royal
Beaufort

Paris
Is.   St.Helena Is.

Port
Hilton Royal ✖ Ft.Beauregar
Head   Sound
Plantation ✖ Ft.Walker

Bluffton

Hilton Head Is.

May
R.

**PORT ROYAL,
HILTON HEAD,
DAUFUSKIE &
SAVANNAH**

Bull Is.

Callibogue
Channel

Daufuskie
Island

ATLANTIC OCEAN

(map by the author)

Savannah R.

Savannah

✖ Ft.Pulaski

Tybee Is.

Little Tybee Is.

The 48th New York on dress review while in garrison. Fort Pulaski, Georgia.

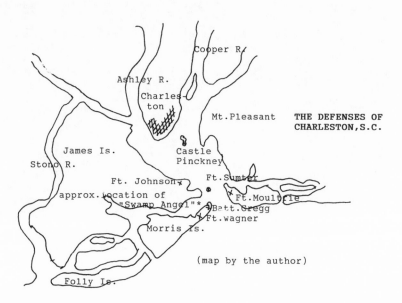

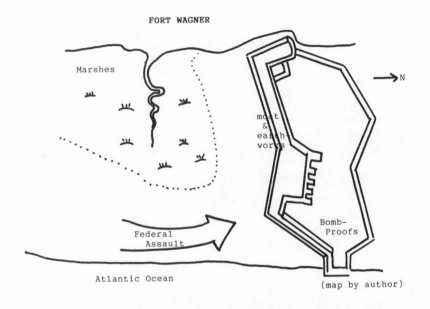

FORT WAGNER

Marshes

moat & earth-works

→ N

Federal Assault

Bomb-Proofs

Atlantic Ocean

(map by author)

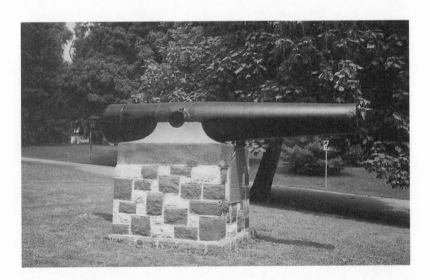

The Swamp Angel as it stands in Trenton, New Jersey, today.
(photo by author)

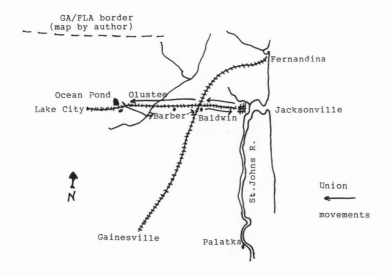

GA/FLA border
(map by author)

Fernandina

Ocean Pond   Olustee

Lake City   Barber   Baldwin   Jacksonville

St.Johns R.

N

Union

movements

Gainesville   Palatka

Petersburg, Virginia: entrenchments and abatis. (photo by author)

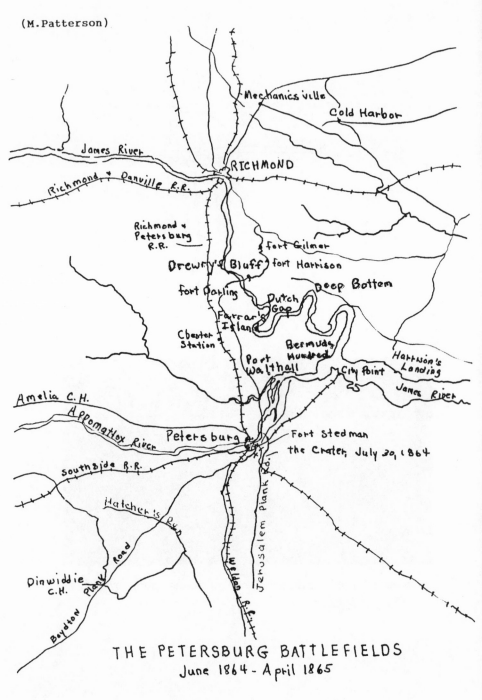

(M. Patterson)

THE PETERSBURG BATTLEFIELDS
June 1864 - April 1865

0   2   4   6   8   10 miles

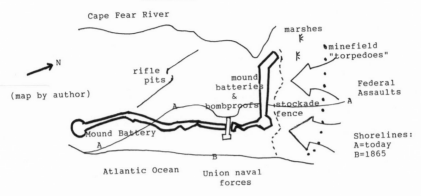

FT.FISHER, N.C.

Cape Fear River

marshes

minefield
"torpedoes"

N

(map by author)

rifle
pits

mound
batteries
&
bombproofs

stockade
fence

Federal
Assaults

A

A

A

Mound Battery

A

B

Shorelines:
A=today
B=1865

Atlantic Ocean

Union naval
forces

This is the bottom portion of the May 7, 1865 letter William
sent to Maggie.

CHAPTER ONE

1861 & 1862

New York to Hilton Head

After training at Camp Wyman in Fort Hamilton, New York, the 48th New York State Volunteers entered combat operations off the Carolina Coast in the fall of 1861.

On April 19, 1861 the Union blockade had been declared by President Lincoln, but it had little immediate impact due to a paucity of naval vessels. The United States Navy had forty-two ships to patrol a Confederate coastline over 3,000 miles long with almost 200 inlets, ports, harbors and river mouths. Nonetheless, Union naval commanders began to facilitate the blockade by taking key forts and islands along the Rebel coastline, always within striking distance of principal Confederate ports. Among these staging areas were Port Royal and Hilton Head Island, South Carolina and Fort Pulaski, Georgia. The 48th NYSV would be stationed at all three of these sites at one time or another during the war. In addition, the targeting of Hatteras Inlet and Roanoke Island, as well as New Bern, North Carolina, New Orleans, Charleston, and even the MacClellan's famed Peninsula Campaign against Richmond in 1862, are evidence of this Union effort to pinpoint choice locations along the Confederate coastline and enhance naval operations with military occupation. The Civil War's coastal campaign was the finest example of combined naval-military operations until World War II.

Much has been debated about the effectiveness of the Union blockade. In my view, the coastal campaign is one of the forgotten theaters of the war and one of the keys to the Federal victory. Stephen R. Wise, in his *Lifeline of the Confederacy,* argues against this premise. Consider the numbers. Estimates range from 6,300 to 8,200 ships that successfully ran the blockade. If one accepts the high-end figure, then this means that not even six ships entered all Southern ports on any given day during the war years. Add to this the sense of gradual strangulation as only one-in-fourteen ships were stopped by the blockade in 1861, one-in-eight in 1862, one-in-four in 1863, one-in-three in 1864 and one-in-two in 1865. Plus, how many of these ships were viable cargo vessels capable of feeding the hungry South? Wise makes an excellent point when he states that the Confederate government failed to mandate the import of military supplies. Therefore, left in the hands of private shippers, the blockade runners more often smuggled higher-priced consumer goods.

I might also suggest that we go directly to the sources such as Mary Chestnut's famed diary or letters such as those in this collection which describe a South desperate for life's material necessities as well as military supplies. Notwithstanding the military successes on the field, the South was conquered in part by being choked off as port after port fell and inlet after inlet was closed.

On October 29, the 48th NYSV sailed from Fortress Monroe off the tip of the York-James Peninsula to rendezvous with a fleet of over 50 vessels before heading south. Linking up on October 29 and surviving a storm off Cape Hatteras in which four ships foundered, the fleet arrived off Port Royal, South Carolina. Port Royal Inlet, north of Hilton Head Island, was strategically significant because of its midpoint location between Savannah and Charleston. In control of this area, Union land and naval forces would be in position for jump-off attacks on both ports.

Flag Officer Samuel F. DuPont set about the task of reducing the two forts guarding Port Royal Inlet at its northern and southern land points. With fifteen ships and 148 guns, he adopted the innovative approach of steaming in an elliptical pattern between the forts, circling and pounding each with broadside fire for some five hours. Not only were the gunships able to reload and keep up a steady rate of fire, but also they presented moving targets for the

Confederate defenders. Fort Walker on the south side of the inlet and Fort Beauregard on the north side eventually surrendered. The date was November 7, 1861. E. Milby Burton, in his *The Siege of Charleston*, appropriately calls this battle "the first major Union victory of the war."[1] Federal troops, over 12,000 strong under Thomas W. Sherman, took possession of Hilton Head Island and erected Fort Mitchel. Meanwhile the navy was able to incorporate Port Royal Sound into their emerging blockade network.

The letters that follow capture some of the early enthusiasm for war, the pride the men felt in their new home, Company D of the 48th NYSV, as well as their involvement in the building of fortifications and their first fight.

Camp Wyman Co. D.
Fort Hamilton
Undated
My Dear Sister,

I thought I would write you a few lines. Things are beginning to look like something. Now we have everything but our guns. More than half of the regiment is made already...half of our company is from New Jersey. I send my love to you all and I expect to see you soon.

Thomas Jones

---

[1] E. Milby Burton, *The Siege of Charleston, 1861-1865* (Columbia, SC: University of South Carolina Press, 1970) 75.

Camp Wyman Company D
Fort Hamilton
August 22, 1861
My Dear Sister,

I would have come home with George Patterson, but I was waiting for a letter from you. I have just received it this evening. I am glad that you are all well and I hope you will remain so. I am also very glad that I am going to have company soon from my own neighborhood, although I feel myself very much at home. Our company is all from New Jersey except a few from Connecticut who came with another company and wished to stay in ours. Today there is not one in the company I would be afraid to sleep with; all are decent looking young men. There was a man who went with the Colonel the other day and said he wanted to join a decent company. So the Colonel brought him to our Captain, and said "Here is a man who wished to join the best company in the Regiment and I brought him to you, knowing that you had a decent company. The regiment I told you about how the other day who went to the fort to guard the prisoners left this afternoon for Washington. I went down to see them go on board the steamer. They had a beautiful band of music, and I tell you it was a nice sight to see them leave in such nice order. Most of their friends came to bid them goodbye, and the boys said it was first rate. One fine fellow hailed up his rifle and said, "Here is the death of Jefferson Davis' boys". We don't expect to leave here in over a month. The regiment leaves New York tomorrow at four o'clock for Washington, We have received our equipment from top to toe. Some of the soldiers that have been in the army for several years say they never saw such fine clothes on soldiers before. If you see George Patterson you can see the suit like we all have. Everything is of a good quality. All of us like our officers first rate. They are fine men. My pay came from the time I first penned down my name. Tell the boys that they will receive pay from the date of enlistment and their fare will be paid back to them again, no matter if they came 500 miles. If you write to me as soon as this comes to hand, let me know if the boys are coming on Monday. I would either come home on Saturday or meet them at the boat on Monday and accompany them down to the camp. I will come home if they will come over with me. Likely, they may put at after one or two days longer. Just write and let me know. It is raining very hard here this evening. I must bring my letter to a close; it is now time the lights are out. We have soap and towels and tobacco and some newspapers. Some have got hymn books and testaments. No more at present. I send my love to you all, hoping to see you all before long.

From Your Affectionate Brother,
Thomas Jones

Camp Wyman
Fort Hamilton
September 14, 1861
My Dear Sister,

I received your letter and present and I was very glad of it. I can not write you but a few lines now. I will write you a long letter the next time I write. William says he will send father's boots home when he sends all the rest of the clothes home. Our band of music came here yesterday. There was a great ball here the night before William Corlies arrived. Our Company is all full[2] and we expect to

---

[2] A "full company" would have meant about 100 men including officers. The table of organization for the Union Army called for about 1000 men to comprise a regiment, although the effective combat strength rarely exceeded 500 men. Four regiments would make up a brigade and two or three brigades comprised a division; three divisions generally made up a corps. Usually three to five corps composed an army, although Union armies in the eastern theaters of the war tended to be larger than those in the west. The Confederate armies employed a similar table of organization,

leave here on Monday morning for Hempstead, about 18 miles from here.[3]

Fort Hamilton
September 1861
Dear Sister,

I thought I could not better apply myself than to write to you this rainy night. I am lonesome now. I have had a good time since I have been here going to the camps to see the boys, but my fun is over now. I saw the boys last night for the last time. They all went away this morning at 4 o'clock in good spirits. They all went on the _____ but no one knows where. _____ knows but he would not tell them. He called them all together yesterday. He told them to pack up and be ready to march at 7 o'clock. At 7 o'clock, I went down. They had their suppers then and they were ready for the march. I do not know whether they all got their uniforms or not. David G. did not have his last night. At 8 o'clock William came with me to the gate. I gave him my ring and one pocket handkerchief. I wished for money to give him [but] I had none. William was well but Thomas was not very well. I saw them all take their suppers, dry bread and coffee was all they had. It made my heart ache to see them all take their suppers. David Corlies said he was going to swear he was married for they were going to leave all the married men to guard the camps. He was making fun for them all. He said he wished he had joined the West Farms Home Guard. He marched with a blanket around his head. He says when he comes back from the wars he is going to get

---

although numerically their corps were often larger. Each division in each army would have an artillery brigade.

[3] The regiment sailed from New York aboard the steamer *John Porter*, marched through Baltimore, and arrived in Washington late on September 18th.

someone to ride him around and show him his old tracks. He won't walk a step. He wonders what West Farms will be like when he comes back. John D.C. and Thomas and William and Woodside and T_____ Broor and David Corlies are all going to bunk together. Their butter was all gone when they went away. George P. got the present of two large cakes and a nice book yesterday morning. He kept the cakes but he left the book with me and one shirt and an umbrella to send home when I could. The boys all wanted me to write today and send their love to all their folks. They did not know where they was going nor when they would have a chance to write. Tell Mr. Patterson what I have got of George's. He sent his love to his folks and you all. Colonel Perry got the present of a beautiful horse yesterday afternoon. Tell Mars Mansfield, David Brasses is well and looks first rate. The men who were on guard on Sunday night shot a woman. She was a German and so was the guard. They shot her. I must soon close for it is late now. Thomas said he saved enough to mail a letter. Poor boys, if they only had money. William kept the books. They think they will get money when they go to Washington. The steamer left the wharf at 7 o'clock this morning. I am not very well this night. I will bring my letter to a close. Give my love to all the folks.

Your Sister Till Death,
Mary Jane

Washington
September 22, 1861
Dear Sister,

I started from Ft. Hamilton on Tuesday morning for Washington. Got in Philadelphia after dark. We had supper of the very best. Then we got on board the cars for Baltimore. We got in Baltimore about twelve o'clock the next day. We were ordered to load our guns.[4] I felt better since I came here than I ever felt before. We got to Washington on Wednesday night. Stayed there all night. Next day we started for camp. Calvin Havens arrived here Saturday. We did not expect him. I came here without a cent in my pocket. No difference. I can do without it. I must leave now. It is dress parade. I will finish after dark. We expect to go on a long march on a secret expedition. In about ten days we expect a large fight. We were encamped right by the New Jersey[ans]. We went over and saw Steifan Lane and John Brown. The boys are all well and hearty.

Your affectionate brother,
William Jones

Washington: Headquarters
Camp Sherman
September, 1861
My Dear Sister,

After a long silence I thought that I would let you know how we are all getting along. I believe that William let you know how we got here and that we had a fine supper in Philadelphia. We then came on through Baltimore and marched with our pieces all loaded. Then we got to Washington yesterday evening. We are camped in a field where there are about 7000 men and 1500 horses. There is one regiment of artillery here with six horses to one cannon.

---

[4] A Baltimore mob attacked the 6th Mass. enroute through their city on April 16. The troops fired back and four soldiers, twelve civilians died (McPherson, 155).

Your Affectionate Brother Til Death,
Thomas Jones

Hilton Head, South Carolina[5]
November 17, 1861
My Dear Sister,

I take my pen in hand to inform you that we are all well at present, and I hope that these few lines find you engaging the same blessing. You write your letters too short. I want to know how Haddie is, and if she goes to school or not.

Well now, I want to let you know a little about things around here. Well, when we were aboard the vessel, we had a very rough time of it indeed, but now we fare a little better here in camp. We are very contented here. We feel safe. There are about 13,000 men besides the artillery and cavalry. Jeff Davis said that if the Yankees got this island, he was in a manner done for. It was the second best fortification he had. They had plenty of help and some of the best cannon that can be found. Well, on the 7th of November 1860, the Stars and Stripes was taken down off the main building on the edge of the shore. It was hauled down by 12 rebels and they swore that the Stars and Stripe should never wave there again. They trampled the flag in the sand. So their rebel flag waved there for one year. On the 7th of November 1861, the battle commenced. I believe it lasted over five hours. So it was just one year to a day from when they trampled our flag in the sand till it waved on the building again.

Well, I was not on hand to see the rebels run or fight, but it was told by them that did see it as an awful sight. One of the Manamass

---

[5] After the Battle of Port Royal Sound, Union troops occupied Hilton Head Island. The 48th New York was stationed there on garrison duty. An unexplained gap in correspondence appears at this point as only four letters survive in the collection from November, 1861 until March, 1862.

men told me he saw one rebel officer hold their flag in one hand and his sword in the other and he stuck just as long as they fought.

Well, a slave that stayed behind said, "When dat big ship went bum, bum, bum, den Massa, he run and his son got killed. Young Massa John got his leg broke [but he was] able to run through the woods and [I] don't know when Massa will get back."

Well, they hauled off the killed and wounded in wagons and they didn't bury but a few. We have prisoners. The slave says there were 5,000 rebels on the other side of the island coming to their assistance, but as soon as they saw their companies run, they turned around. And they were going by steam to see who could get off the island first. We found cannon balls that our vessels threw about two miles from the shore.

There is lots of corn, sweet potatoes, and cotton here. The rebels bragged that on account of their good crops, they could have stayed a great deal longer. Colonel Sorell's regiment is here. William and I saw Frank Halpern. He was the only one I knew in the regiment. John Jones, John Learden and Stiles are in New York. The boys are all in good spirits. David Corlies, William, J.S., Y.C., J.P.S., P.H. Smith, and Havens are all well. D. Brassels is well. He had a letter the other day. It said Y.P. Hall got his leg broken into pieces and was dangerously ill. Address your letter to Fort Sullivan, 48th New York Volunteers. The men next to us got paid off yesterday, and we are to get paid off tomorrow.

I send you a little specimen of cotton. I do not cook any more on the account that I was losing all my drill. J.P. is stout so therefore we had a nice time eating beef and chickens.

No more at present, but remaining your brother till death,

Thomas Jones.

SO KEEP A LOOK OUT FOR THE NEXT LETTER. DON'T LET ANY ONE SEE THIS ONE FOR I EXPECT TO SEND MY MONEY WHETHER IN A BOOK OR IN A LETTER.

Hilton Head, South Carolina
January 6, 1862
My Dear Sister,

I take my pen in hand to inform you of our whereabouts, health, and so on. Well, all of the boys have their health first rate-except myself. I have been sick for better than a week, but not so [much] as to be in the hospital. I have kept to my tent all the time and I am now getting well. I trust you will hear a good many rumors about the battle our regiment was into on New Year's Day but you need not believe everything you hear. They left here on New Year's Eve and went to a place about 25 miles from here by the name of Port Royal Ferry. We landed on New Year's Day. There was a woods a little over a mile from the shore to the ferry where we landed. Our company was sent out as skirmishers to find out what was in the woods. They went right up within a few yards of a masked battery. The rebels fired a great deal of canister and shell and musketry right at the 48th. They supposed they had killed all of the Yankees, but just as quick as our boys saw smoke we hid. You see, our company was so close to them they could hear the Rebels give orders. We heard the Rebels give the order to fire. So just as quick as our boys saw smoke from their cannon, we all fell down in the cotton furrows. They said the balls flew around them like hailstones. They could hear the Rebels give the order "give the damned Yankees more shell". So we rose up and fired on the battalion and never lost a man. Then the gunboats went to throwing shells into them. Our boys say it was awful to hear the cry of the wounded in the woods. A Rebel officer came with a flag of truce and wanted us to stop and give them two hours to bury their dead. One of our men went too close to them. They took him prisoner. So our General told him he would give them four hours to bury the dead, only if he brought back the prisoner. So they brought back the prisoner to our men. Our men say they had four horse teams hauling away the dead for several hours. Our captain asked the general how many men he lost. Said he, "You wouldn't believe me if I told you". I was not there. I was sick and could not go. They thought of going again in a few days. I am now getting well so I think I will be able to go the next time. I heard mother worried and fretted a good deal about us. Tell her she must not fret so. I think we will all get home safely. It seems to me that if there was going to be anyone killed they would have been killed on New Year's Day. But we may get in a tighter _____ than that was.

Remain Your Affectionate Brother Til Death,
Thos. Jones

Hilton Head, South Carolina
January 11, 1862

Thursday afternoon. I take my pen in hand as I have a good opportunity to do it today so I thought that I could improve my wasted time and write a few lines to you. I should like to hear from you and I think that it would be the best way to write you and then I should get an answer. We have been into a battle at Port Royal Ferry and the bullets flew all around us but they did not hit us at all. We laid flat upon the ground while the bullets were flying. We burned their buildings and then left the spot after taking quite a good deal of their property. I think that we will go and give them another turn. We fought long. They are regular cowards for they dare not come out and have a fair fight. The cowardly dogs, they stay hid in the woods and when they get a shy chance to shoot someone they would sneak out like a snake and that is the reason that we cannot shoot them. I think that we will give them long _____ pretty soon so that they will be glad to come out and surrender. I think that we will all live to see the time that we will all be home to see each other again and sport and play as we have in days that are past and gone. I think perhaps that I have written enough and it is getting time for me to stop. Please write soon and tell me how the war fever raged in West Farms.

Unsigned

CHAPTER TWO

1862 & 1863

Savannah to Charleston

On February 1, 1862 the 48th landed and encamped on Daufuskie Island near the mouth of the Savannah River and adjacent to Hilton Head Island. Initially, the coastal expedition had been under the command of General William T. Sherman, but he was replaced by General David Hunter. There is a bit of an incongruity in some of the initial letters as a subsequent letter is dated March 8 and seems to indicate that Hunter is in command. The regimental history notes that Hunter took over on March 31. He immediately commenced operations aimed at taking Ft. Pulaski and accomplished this on April 11, 1862. The Jones brothers had been involved in the support operations on nearby Daufuskie Island.

The 48th was then sent into garrison duty inside Ft. Pulaski. There are two excellent wartime photographs of the 48th on review inside the fort. In addition, the reduction of Ft. Pulaski is noteworthy in and of itself. The Fort was considered impregnable to solid shot cannon fire with its seven-and-one-half foot thick masonry walls. Moreover, the range factor placed the fort somewhat out of harms' way for guns heavy enough to pound the fort into submission. Therefore, Union batteries employed rifled cannonry and concentrated their fire at a specific point along the fort's southeastern walls and rampart. In so doing they not only forced open a breach in the wall but also threatened to blow up the powder magazine situated at that corner of the fort.

The city of Savannah was over ten miles away and the rebel garrison under Colonel Charles H. Olmstead was cut off. His walls breached and under fire from Quincy A. Gillmore's three dozen guns on nearby Tybee Island, Olmstead had little choice but to surrender the fort and its 385-man contingent. Although there was little actual loss of life, Gillmore's use of rifled cannon forced a change in the conventional wisdom of the day. His guns, with their increased accuracy, greater range and deeper penetrating capabilities, showed that such ordnance could indeed reduce heavy masonry forts such as Pulaski. Savannah remained cut off from the sea for the rest of the war although the city itself did not fall to Union forces until William Tecumseh Sherman completed his famous March to the Sea on December 21, 1864.

Gillmore's report, later published in volume two of *Battles and Leaders of the Civil War*, states that his guns fired 5,275 rounds at the fort, some from a distance of 3,400 yards.[6]

Fort Pulaski is in excellent preservation today and is a fine example of the "System III Fortifications," a series of heavy coastal defenses built in the decades just before the Civil War. Fort Sumter and Fort Delaware are other good examples of these multi-tiered, masonry fortifications. They served to replace earthen works such as Fort McHenry, a fine example of a System II fortification built in the years just after the turn of the 19th century. America has always been concerned with its coastal defenses and one can even look at the revampings inside the System III forts to see upgrades on the eve of the Spanish-American War. For instance, inside Ft. Sumter and nearby Ft. Moultrie can be seen black-coated, elongated concrete structures that were built to increase the durability of these older forts. They may ruin the view for many a Civil War buff, but it is important to understand the mindset that created them. Fort Pulaski is devoid of such additional accouterments except for a large tree that now grows in the middle of the parade ground.

The collection of letters in this chapter provide are filled with a range of emotions. The opening correspondence offers a sense that

---

[6] Clarence Clough Buel, Robert Underwood Johnson, Editors, *Battles and Leaders of the Civil War* (Edison, NJ: Castle Publishers) 2:10.

the war will end soon, a hope that is dashed by the end of the chapter when war weariness is all too evident in the brothers' letters home. They also experience the loss of their regimental commander. Furthermore, it is in the timeframe of these letters that the Emancipation Proclamation is issued, changing the tone of the war and leading to a dismal sense of betrayal within many Union soldiers, including the Jones brothers.

Fort Pulaski, Georgia
February 3, 1862[7]
Dear Sister Maggie,

I take my pen in hand this evening to let you know that we are well and I hope this will find you all enjoying the same blessing. I will give you the news of the day as near as I can. General Foster from North Carolina is here with all his force and there is more expected every day. General Corferin is expected here with his force everyday. General Foster and General Hunter came here to the fort today to pay us a visit. It is the first time I ever saw them. They are fine looking men. There are three ironclads here. They have been trying to take a battery a little below us now for a few days. The Rebels think that we can't take it, but they will find out when we commence. In earnest, they struck one of the ironclads one day last week with over 30 shots and they rolled right off her – never hurt in the least, so I guess they were only trying the rebels to see what they could do with them. I think when all our force gets here in a few days this department can muster at the least 50 or 60,000 men. So you see, by the time you receive this letter, there will likely be some very heavy fighting going on in this department. I don't know whether we will leave the fort or not. As yet, I don't see any sign of it. We have just received this morning and last evening an account

---

7 Ft. Pulaski did not fall to Union forces until April 11, so these letters must emanate from encampments on Daufuskie Island or Tybee Island since both were involved in the siege operations.

from Charleston harbor. It runs as follows: it appears there was an English ship trying to run in the harbor. She was loaded with plating and machinery engines and in fact a complete outfit for two iron clads and two million dollars of specie on board besides several other valuable stores. She had on board a steam machine for molding rifled cannon balls and the man that invented it. The vessel and its cargo was valued at six million dollars. Six million dollars is the largest prize that has ever been captured at any one time since the war commenced. She lays now in Port Royal harbor in our possession. The Rebs ran out to her in ironclad rams to try to assist her in running off the sand. One of our wooden gun boats disabled the gunboat named *Paul Jones*. She has put out to sea and has not been heard of yet. Some think she has gone to the bottom and some think that she has got on track of another vessel. Anyhow, the Rebels put in again. They didn't accomplish what they came out for. We can put two more iron boats together in a very short time. We have not been paid off yet. I think we will be paid off before this month is out, as the troops have nearly all been paid except those in this department. The weather here now is very changeable. One day is warm and nice and the next rains or is as cold as Greenland. This month, I think, will be all the winter we will have down here. In fact, the farmers begin to plant here the first of this month. You must write soon and often as you can. You will get this in the course of a week from this date. I will try and write you another one on the ninth.

Your brother,
Thomas

Fort Pulaski, Georgia
March 8, 1862
Dear Sister Maggie,

I seat myself down to send you a few lines to let you know that we are all well and hoping that these few lines will find you all the same. Today is Sunday and Thomas is on guard. I will be on tomorrow.

I have a ring to send to Haddie in remembrance of me. I don't know of any news to send you today, only that we are not going on that expedition the generals want us to go on. General Hunter says that we must stay in here till Charleston is taken. I read that they would not put a green regiment in the fort to let it fall in the hands of Rebels as he knows that it will be attacked as soon as we attack Charleston.

I would like to know why you don't receive my letters. I wish you would write more often if you please. All the directions you need fill in as Mr. William Jones, Co. D 48 Reg., N.Y.S.V., Fort Pulaski, Georgia. That is all; there is no use of putting too much on.

Tell Haddie that this ring is for her to keep in remembrance of me till this war is ended.

Maggie take good care of my wagon till I come home.

I may close for the present. Give my best respect to all.

Goodbye From William Jones

Ft. Pulaski, Georgia
March 11, 1862
Maggie,

William and David C. and J.D. and all the rest of the boys are first rate. Now then, when you read these two letters, I think you will excuse me for not writing you sooner. We have one or two gunboats out in the Savannah River. Also we have a battery on each side of the river now. I don't wonder if before you receive this letter we will have Ft. Pulaski in our possession but it is a long ride and a strong fort and I have no doubt it will be a hard place to take.

I understand that two Rebels came down yesterday from the city of Savannah to one of our gunboats and asked the Captain's protection, but I have not heard yet what they had to say as the officers took them down in the hole to question them. I have no doubts at all but they will give a good deal of information. It is very nice weather down here now. The orange and lemon trees are in bloom. Try and let me know how father is getting along-let me know if he wants a little money to get hay or something else.

From your brother, Thomas
Yours til death
Goodbye!

Daufuskie Island, Georgia
March 11, 1862
My Dear Sister,

I take my pen in hand after a long silence to let you know that I am well at present. David Corlies, William, John Woodside and myself, us four, tent together. We have got new tents and we have plenty of room. J.D. Cottrell and Christopher Brewer do the cooking for us. I suppose you have heard all about our moving from Hilton Head and going aboard of that unlucky steamship the *Winfield Scott*, the same one that lost her rigging and masts coming here. We were sailing from Hilton Head in the direction of Savannah and we got laid high and dry on Long Pine Island. She broke right in two in the middle. We all got off safely and we had a nice time of it running around the island, shooting Seesesh cattle[8] and cooking them. There was plenty of them and as we had no fresh beef in a good long while, we sailed right in, but why do I linger so long about anything so old? The shipwreck you may have heard about. Well, when we came to Daufuskie Island they set us to work carrying pine poles on our shoulders about the distance from one and one half to two miles. There were 20,000 poles and we carried them in nine days. One of our companies was out on duty so there was only eight companies to do the work. When this was done, we had to haul eight large cannon across a marsh over a mile long. Then and there we built a battery to

---

8 "Seesesh" was a common slang reference among Union soldiers; it was short for secessionist. The word was often spelled "secesh."

command the Savannah River. When we were hauling the cannon across the marsh we had two small planks for them to run on and once and a while they would run off the track and sink in the mud clear up to the hub. It was done mostly at night. The Rebels would sail down the Savannah right past our boxes and we would lay down or squat in the cane or bullrushes till they got past. They never knew we were there till we got our guns mounted and ready to play on them. Then came the fun of throwing up the entrenchments around the cannons to protect the gunners. We could only work at low tide. At high tide the water would be from knee to waist deep, and sometimes, it would be raining like everything. A big raft of fat pine logs came floating down the river just about the time our boys wanted some firewood. They kindled a fire and then when the tide rose it took the fire afloat on the raft! When we went to the battery we would stay up there one night and a day or I might say 24 hours, except for the last time. Our company stayed eight days before we got relieved. Now at this present time we have to go on guard duty about every other day. We have hardly a moment to spare for anything.[9]

Thomas Jones

---

[9] General Quincy Gillmore's official report states that the men of the 48th, along with men from the 7th Connecticut, lugged some 1900 poles over a mile of marshland to build a wharf on nearby Jones Island. This was completed on Feb. 4. Then the men were assigned the arduous task of pushing, pulling and straining the guns across the marshes onto and into what would eventually be five batteries on Tybee Island.

To Maggie E. Jones
Daufuskie Island
April 1, 1862
Dear Parents,

I take my pen in hand to let you know that I am just well at the present, hoping that these few lines will find you the same. I have been sick for a few days but today I feel much better. I had the fever.

I have something to tell you about what I dreamt last night. I thought I was digging marl on that bank of Winsor's on the line behind David _____. I was loading wagons. I thought I saw into the hole – father and James P. Johnson. I thought the bank cracked about 10 feet back. I saw it and gave the alarm. Someone in the hole yelled, "Oh God Almighty, the bank is all caving in and there is no way to get out" and with that I woke up and I was all wet with sweat. So I heard around that Cate Woolley got married. Let me know who.

You're the same love here as before. The weather is getting warm.

From your brother,
William Jones

Daufuskie Is., Georgia
May 15, 1862
My Dear Sister,

We have heard of the retreat by the Rebels on the peninsula of Yorktown.[10] I suppose you have heard of it too. A few days ago we saw one of the Rebel gunboat flag ships. She was manned mostly with niggers. The niggers tied what white men they had on board and ran the ship out to our blockading fleet and surrendered.[11]

---

[10] The comment on Yorktown refers to George McClellan's Peninsula Campaign in Virginia; the Jones brothers were not part of this operation.

[11] The incident Thomas is referring to actually happened in Charleston. The steamer *Planter* was hijacked by Robert Smalls and a slave crew on

Our men put a few men on board and she steamed into Hilton Head. She is in Hilton Head now. The Rebels up here in Savannah have been communicating with our general with a flag of truce everyday. I believe they are going to surrender to us.

Part Second
May 21, 1862

John Walt is dead. He died in the hospital on Sunday, the 18th and he was buried on the same day. He died of the fever. He suffered a great deal and when he was dead he looked nothing like himself at all.

We are yet on Daufuskie Island and there is no sign of getting away but if we have to stay in the army this summer I would rather stay here than anywhere else for it is sandy and warm and healthy. I believe it as fine an island as any in the South. Our guard duty has been every night. I will be awaiting to hear of what luck our boys have at Yorktown and Richmond and I think if we gain those three battles that it will nearly bring the war to a close.

Thomas Jones

Hilton Head, South Carolina
June 1, 1862
Dear Parents,

As today is Sunday I thought I would write you a few lines to let you know how we are all getting along. Well, eight companies of ours moved away from the fort for the period of one or two months. Where we are going I can't tell. We struck tents here last night and the boys seem to like it very well.

Well, I suppose you heard of the Rebel ram in Savannah last Wednesday the 17th. This month the ram *Atlanta* ran out of

---

May 12. Reaching the Union blockade ships, she was impounded and taken to Hilton Head.

Savannah by way of Savannah Sound. About a week ago there was a deserter from Savannah who informed us that the ram was going to run out so Commander DuPont dispatched nine monitors up there. She ran aground and put up a white flag. I saw them fighting on Wednesday morning. I am well at present; address just the same as before.

From William Jones

Fort Pulaski, Georgia
June 5, 1862
Part the 2nd

We can all look ahead to the great battle that is expected at Richmond and we expect to hear of one at Corinth every day.[12] We all think that if we gain the day at those two places the war will soon be to an end. It seems a very short time since I enlisted.

Calvin Havins was transferred to Company F and J[ohn] Marks transferred to Company B. Neither one had very good officers. They did not use their men well and of course their men did not like them. Calvin did something that put him in the guard house. They kept him in over a month but they couldn't prove anything against him

---

[12] Following the battle of Shiloh in April, Union forces under Gen. Henry Halleck pressed Confederate General P.G.T. Beauregard's army southward into northeastern Mississippi. Beauregard abandoned Corinth early in June. This battle, along with the fight at Iuka, has come to be seen as an early yet critical engagement. Corinth, Mississippi lies astride the Memphis-to-Charleston railroad that was referred to as the "backbone of the South". The north-south Mobile & Ohio tracks also ran though the city. On May 30, 1862 Union forces under William Rosecrans occupied the vacant city as Beauregard had withdrawn to Tupelo. When the latter attempted to re-take Corinth in October, he failed and lost nearly one-quarter of his 22,000 men in doing so. Historians now see the Confederate failures at Antietam, Perryville, and Corinth as a combined turning point in the war as they all occurred in the late summer and fall of 1862.

and they had to let him out. We have half-rations of fresh bread and half of crackers. We have been alone for some time now.

So Good bye.
Unsigned

Fort Pulaski, Georgia
June 10, 1862
Sister Maggie,

Everything is doing fine here. They are building up the fort every day, hauling cannon around and shipping them [to] different places. Some are going over on [to] Tybee Island......loading shot and shell on a schooner – that is a small ship. Some are going up [to] Jones Island on picket duty in the evening. We have dress parade in the evening. Yesterday I was over on Tybee Island helping to load shot and shell on their vessel. The wind blew very hard and the river was very rough. We had a large rowboat and we got stuck fast on the _____.

Well, I bet you have smiled if you had seen about twenty of us get into water and mud over our knees and haul the boat along.

This is the way time passes down here.

Your Brother Till Death,
Thomas Jones

Fort Pulaski, Georgia
June 10, 1862
Dear Sister,

I take my pen in hand to let you know that we are all well at present and hoping that these few lines will find you all the same. We got paid the other day and I will send it in this letter. I want you to get that wagon as soon as possible. I will not write much this time. There is nothing new to write; all is the same, only that our troops are about to take Charleston. We have lost one of our company, his name was James Herbert.

Remain your affectionate brother till death.
William Jones

Fort Pulaski, Georgia
June 10, 1862
My Dear Sister,

I take my pen in hand once more to inform you that we are all well as usual and I hope that those few lines may find you all the same. William has just sent father twenty dollars. We expect our Colonel to go home soon but we do not know the exact time. We received mail here last night be we got no letters. Cal Havins got a letter from his brother, John Havins. I heard it read. I am glad to hear that he is well.

J.D. Cottrell, J.A. Woodside, Christopher Brewer, A. Hires, David Brassel, [and] Calvin Havens are all doing well. We are quartered in the fort and we like it first rate. We get fresh bread almost every day. We have had a very long, cold storm. I want you to write more often to us and let us know all the news. Put three postage stamps when you send me one. There is good news coming into camp every mail. We have heard that the Rebels are leaving Corinth and of the fighting that was done near Richmond. I think that the Rebels are getting all in a body so our army will make a short job of it. Now I believe that the war is close to an end. The Rebels are nearly played out and there are so many coming over into Union lines that is what makes me think that the war is nearly over. Calvin Havins is out of the guardhouse and alright again. They could not prove anything against him.

No more at present
but remain your affectionate brother till death.
Thomas Jones

Head-Quarters,
48th Regiment, N.Y.S.V. Co. D
Fort Pulaski, Georgia
June 20, 1862
My Dear Sister,

I have just received your letter bearing the date of June 9th. I am glad to hear that you are all well. William got a letter and I got two papers from you. We are all well as usual. We had a very heavy storm three days ago. A sutler's vessel[13] was blown ashore here and was wrecked. He lost nearly everything he had. William and I have sent home twenty dollars each.

Our camp this morning is a camp of mourning. We have lost our best friend and Colonel, James H. Perry. Yesterday, the 19th, he departed this life. He was in our quarter only the day before he died. He ate a hardy dinner and then he dropped off so suddenly that when John Woodside came in and said our Colonel was dead, none of us believed him. We all feel it is a very heavy loss. I don't know what we will do now. We will never replace him.[14]

I hope you will excuse all mistakes. Write as soon as this comes to hand. We are going to start with the Corps at ten o'clock today for New York.

Thomas Jones to his sister,
Maggie E. Jones

---

[13] Sutlers were itinerant merchants who traveled with army regiments to offer for sale items like paper, ink, clothing, sewing needles, etc.

[14] According to the regimental history, Col. Perry died of a stroke in the afternoon of the 18th. Bell Wiley elaborates on a slightly different angle. "In June 1862 while this unit was stationed on Tybee Island, a storm blew ashore a large quantity of beer and wine and Perry's Saints proceeded to get gloriously drunk. The incident must have upset the reverend colonel greatly, for he was fatally stricken on the very next day..." (252-253).

Fort Pulaski, Georgia
June 20
Dear Sister Maggie and all the rest of the folks-father, mother
Haddie, all together.

I am sad today. I have just come in from a funeral. I suppose you
say, why is it? No, none of my partners from around home. I must
tell you that the 48th had lost their father, our best friend: our
Colonel is dead, day before yesterday. He ate his dinner as hardy as
ever just before 3 o'clock Sunday and died in the night. This
afternoon they wanted one man out of each company for a body
guard for him. They wanted respectable young men and I was the
one out of our company to go. You know that a man who dies in his
natural health won't keep long. Last night we had to drink whiskey
and other stuff. The doctor told us we must drink it for our own
good. The reason that we had to keep him so long was that they had
to go to Hilton Head to get a coffin and they could not get one big
enough so they had to get a common pine coffin and bury him here.
They will raise him in a few days and send him home. There was a
very big thunder shower last night so this morning we were pretty
well tired out. They were going to make a work detail but the
Lieutenant Colonel said that we had done the most work and we
might as well have the honor of carrying him to the grave. So we
carried our brave commander to his long home. When they raise
him to send him home, we will have a chance to go home to the city
of Brooklyn. That will be a bigger day than any that was here. I think
I will be home before the war is over, yet I don't know. The Colonel
would never see any of his men imposed on. They can't send a man
out of New York to fill his place but they may have filled it here.
When he died, Lieutenant Paxson came out and said, "Boys, your
colonel is dead." There was not a word spoken. We folded up
everything and left work. The 47th of New York is up toward
Charleston. The said that they would not fight nor work anymore if
they could not fight with the 48th and Colonel Perry with them. This

week they had a fight[15] and that most of the other regiments ran and left them alone. They charged on the rebels and got on the parapet. The looked around and saw that they were alone. They hollered out "Oh, where is the 48th?" Ever since the battle of Port Royal they want to be with us all the time. They had to retreat with their losses. The think there is no man in the service like Colonel Perry but his fighting is over. We will miss him if ever we have to go into battle.

William Jones

Letter not headed or addressed
July 5, 1862

I thought I would write you a few lines to inform you that we are all right and well and hope this may find you all enjoying the same great pleasure and blessing. This morning is very cool. We celebrated the 86th anniversary of our independence yesterday at 12 o'clock. There were 30 guns fired in honor of the birth of our freedom and independence. We had fireworks and everybody seemed to enjoy themselves. While we are a great distance from home we do not forget those who are in our homes. We have been very fortunate since we have been in the service for we have not lost a lot of men. Our first lieutenant went to Savannah with a flag of truce and two prisoners last Thursday. I saw both of them and they looked very bad. One had his hand torn off at the wrist. They were both sick and they looked as if they had the cough – they were so thin and faded. The lieutenant asked one of them if they had any money. He replied that had not had any since he enlisted. I think it must go rather hard with them. On Thursday night we had a very heavy thunder storm and the lightning was very sharp. It blinded me at every flash. I suppose that you have heard that our colonel is

---

[15] According to reports, the 47th New York performed gallantly in a brief skirmish on the mainland near Bluffton. About this same time the Battle of Secessionville occurred just outside of Charleston SC, and some New York contingents were involved.

deceased and our captain has resigned his commission.[16] George Patterson is trying for captain in the darkie regiment that has been formed at Hilton Head.[17]

Unsigned

Letter not headed
July 27, 1862
Dear Sister,

I take my pen in my hand to let you know that we are all well at present and we are hoping that these few lines will find you the same. You are in debt to me by half a dozen letters. I have had no letter since I sent that money. You mention that you got it and that was in Thomas' letter.

There is one who has been called away since I come to this fort. David [Corlies] was taken sick and died very suddenly. He had been as healthy as any man in the company. He was sick about two weeks and some days. He got up in the chair and dropped his head and J.D. said, "Dave, you better hold your head up-it may hurt you that way." So he put his hand to his head and he died sitting in the chair. I stood there till he breathed his last. The company misses him.[18] He is missed among us for he was lively and funny. The next day, D.

---

[16] Capt. Daniel C. Knowles resigned in July as Co. D's captain on June 30, 1862; he was replaced by Lt. Paxson.

[17] In August, 1862 the First South Carolina Volunteers cam into being. This was a black regiment of former slaves and freedmen from SC who enlisted under the command of noted abolitionist Col. Thomas Wentworth Higginson. The served in the coastal campaigns from South Carolina to Florida, including service as support troops for the assault on Battery Wagner near Charleston in July 1863.

[18] Many Northern soldiers were unaccustomed to the semi-tropical heat and humidity, not to mention the tropical diseases. Such non-combat fatalities would eventually surpass, in numbers, those inflicted by enemy gunfire. To put it another way, two out of every three Civil War deaths was disease-related.

Emmons and Thomas and me and H. Smith made a fence around his grave and sodded it and Lieutenant Bodine got a headstone. But we don't know who will be the next one of us to be called away. I don't know what the reason is why you don't write.

From your brother till death,
William Jones

Good bye. A word to you Maggie-you can write to others but you can't write to me. You can't cheat me for I can tell your handwriting in amongst a thousand. You need not get offended for I say as I mean.

Thomas took it upon himself to write a letter of condolence to David Corlies' sister, Elizabeth.

Part Second

Dear Friend Elizabeth,

May God help you to stand up under this trouble. If he had been home it would not have been so hard. He could have had a sister to wait on him and supply his wants. He stood it all like a brave soldier [and] never complained of his lot. He was well thought of by his officers and by his brother soldiers. He was always on hand, never shirked his duty. This was his first sickness. Little did I think when we came here that we would leave him here.

Remain Your Friend,
Thomas to E.A. Corlies

Fort Pulaski, Georgia
August 9, 1862
Dear Friend Margaret,

David Corlies died three weeks ago and we miss him a great deal. He was buried with military honors. The salute was by eight of us and he was escorted by the entire company. We have not moved from the fort and do not expect to for quite some time yet and we may not at all for we are considered Regulars. Three or four companies are going to take a battery on one of the islands around here. I do not know where it is for a soldier is not certain of anything until he gets it or does it. A soldier's life is an uncertain one.

Our company was out almost all night on Friday when we got the news that a Rebel ironclad batters was coming down the river to try and run the blockade. There were 24 of our boys arming three guns and ten of us were carrying ammunition. It was quite dark and the battery did not come down [the river after all]. But there was a steamer that tried to run by on Sunday night. She could not proceed as we put two balls in her. She put back and we have not seen or heard anything of her since.

No More At Present
From Your Friend,
John A. Woodside
Co. D, 48 NYSV

Headquarters
Fort Pulaski, Georgia
August 10, 1862
My Dear Sister,

We feel very lonesome since David Corlies has left us. When he was with us, he was the life of the company. I never saw anyone that could enjoy themselves with as little of home as he did. I feel for his folks. You must write to me and let me know how they took it.

I wish you had been down here yesterday to see the fun. There was a Rebel steamer that came down with a flag of truce and fetched a lady and a little boy. Our little steamer went to meet them and took off the boy and his mother. So, the Rebels promised to wait where they were until General Hunter heard of it. They lay in the river about a good gunshot away and General Hunter forbade them from coming here any more with a flag of truce. They only come down to spy around. While our little steamer was down at the dock to unload the lady and her boy, they took the advantage and started double quick for Savannah. Eight cannons opened fire on her but to no use. She was out of range of our guns. Meantime we had a small cannon on the dock. It was put on our little tug and she started after the Rebel steamer.[19] By and by the Rebels had over three miles of a start but our little tug soon got in gunshot of her and fired. She stopped and hove to.

August 12, 1862

We all suppose that the prisoners, of course, would be sent to Hilton Head and from there, to Fort Lafayette or some other line of confinement. We left their steamer here on the night of the 11th and brought them to the fort. We kept a strong guard over them and gave them all they wanted to eat and drink. On the morning of the 12th we took them to Hilton Head to see General Hunter. We thought they were spies and would be punished accordingly but on this same evening, they returned to the steamer and went to Savannah again, but for what reason we cannot find out. The hands on board thought they were treated very well. One of them, when leaving for Hilton Head, proposed three cheers for the 48th and they told us where their plantations were. They said they were sorry such a feeling prevailed between the two parties. They hoped it would soon be settled. They said that when peace was declared they would like to have the 48th pay them a visit.

August 13, 1862

I know it was a sad blow to David's friends to hear of his death but this is a trying time for lots of families that one year ago were merry and happy. Now at this present time they are covered with mourning and the full fare is not told yet. I hear there are 600,000

---

[19] The *General Lee.*

more men coming into the field. If that is so, hope it is and believe that the war will soon be over.

Your Affectionate Brother Till Death,
Thomas Jones[20]
To his sister Maggie E. Jones, Good Bye!

Fort Pulaski Georgia
August 18, 1862
Dear Sister Maggie,

I have just received your kind and welcome letter today and was glad to hear that you are all well. I will get my profile[21] taken and send it home, then I will have time to write a long letter. The boys are all quite well at present. David was not sick over two weeks. Our company came over from Tybee Island. John D. wrote and he hardly had the letter mailed when he died. He was very sensible to the last, sat on the chair and told John D. to send his money home and that was the last. He died sitting in the chair. I never want to see such a sight again as to stand by the side of a partner and see him die. It is something that I never experienced before. I know that if I had known that he was so near gone, I would not have gone in to see him, but we did not know. When I write again, I will tell you about the Rebels. There were some 10 or 12 of them who came down under a flag of truce. Our officers took them to Hilton Head and showed them our troops and the ironclads gun boats.

No more at present.
From your brother William Jones

---

[20] The letters dated August 10, 12, and 13 were all mailed together by Thomas.

[21] William is referring to a cartes de visite, today commonly referred to as a "CDV". These pocket-sized photos made for a 19th century calling card/business card/momento and were very popular.

Letter not headed
September 2, 1862
Dear Friend Maggie,

I wrote you a few times to inform you that we are all well at present and hope you are the same. I was very sorry to hear you were sick. I hope you are a great deal better this time and hope you will continue so for a long time to come. We are all getting along as well as soldiers generally do and a great deal better than some of the soldiers do. We went on to Bull Is. to look for Rebels but did not see any or anything of them. We marched about three miles to a plantation house and it was quite a march for it was very hot. When we got back to the boat, we were wet from head to foot with sweat, but we met with no accident. Thomas and William were not with us, there were only 20 men and they were all of Co. D. While I am sitting here writing, the band is playing a lot. We are going to lose our band for they have been mustered out of service. There is no regimental band allowed by the government. Only brigade bands are allowed[22] and each is composed of 16 men.

No more for present
From your friend,
John A. Woodside
You must excuse this ink for it's some I made myself.

---

[22] In July, 1862 all regimental bands were broken up. There were no musical bands below brigade level (Wiley, 157). It may also be noted that band musicians often were called upon to drop their instruments in favor of stretchers once battle was joined. Individual soldiers were of course allowed to keep their instruments often to the delight of their comrades, as shown by the famous story of the lonely coronet player who serenaded troops on both sides of the trench lines during the siege of Vicksburg.

Fort Pulaski, Georgia
October 3, 1862
Dear Sister,

The left wing of our regiment was called out to fight the enemy at 12 o'clock [p.] m. We loaded our gun boats and went towards Bluffton on the mainland. It was about daylight when we landed. The river was not very wide and it was very foggy on the mainland. There was a picket of cavalry but we could not see them in the fog. We marched about 18 or 19 miles from where we landed.

We came to Bluffton and found it evacuated. We fetched three pianos out of one house that we went in. We went in while the boats shelled the woods. There were about 400 cavalry waiting for us, but the gun boats shelled them so they retreated. We got on the turnpike that leads to Charleston and Savannah. They did not see us but we saw them in an open field and the shells were a-bursting among them like fury, so we returned to the gun boats.

There was as fine a house as I have seen since I came from home but we did not go further for the boats were out of shells. The folks had just left and there was sweet potatoes and sweet milk for dinner. They left it for us. [They also] left a note on the wall that said, "Search our house, you sons of B--." We took all the furniture and left. If we had fought their cavalry, they would have lost half a regiment in one volley. The 48th has a great name. The boys are all well.

From Your Brother Till Death,
William Jones

Fort Pulaski, Georgia
Oct. 20, 1862
My Dear Sister Maggie,

If you remember, I spoke of our colonel going up on the mainland and leaving a black man to spy and see how the Rebels were situated. At the end of five days he was to go get him again.

Well, the fifth day happened to be this last Saturday. Our Colonel got on board the steamer *Planter* and took Co. B with him, the same company that David Brassal is in. They went up to the city of Bluffton and got the spy they left there. What few Rebels they saw ran out of the way as fast as their legs could carry them. They were coming home again and just in the dusk of the evening they got to where the river was very narrow with a very high bluff all covered with woods and brush which was overlooking the river from this spot. They were fired into by a large number of Rebels which lay there concealed. They were not over 50 yards off. If they had been good marksmen, they might have done a good deal of damage.

They wounded one man belonging to Co. B and one mate on the steamer. Our men drove them off by throwing shell and grape into the woods amongst them until it was late and the tide was falling fast. The corporal belonging to Co. B is dead. He will be buried today. The others, it is believed, will get well. It is the first man that the 48th has lost by a Rebel ball, but they have never taken a single prisoner from us.

Camp Monmouth[23]
October 24, [1862]
Dear Margaret,

I received your letter on the 22 and was much pleased. I was on picket duty three miles from camp and in a dangerous and lonesome place when I received your letter along with one from John Coning. There were three of us on one post. We went to a farmer's house and captured some apples and milk, the first I had since I left home.

Our camps are in fine order. We are dressed very well and have plenty of cook's grub. We are working on forts and digging rifle pits. We expect to get our pay in a few days and, if I get my pay, I can send you my profile. The boys are all well. We have a little Bible class every Sabbath and meetings every evening.

---

[23] The author of this letter, John D. Fogerty, was stationed in the ring of forts that surrounded the capital district.

A rebel spy was caught in Washington and marched off under five guards. Washington is a very fine city, but I do not think much of the people. I like the city of Philadelphia better than any place yet.

From Your Schoolmate,
John D. Fogerty

Fort Pulaski, Georgia
October 27, 1862
My Dear Sister,

About eight to ten days ago, our company [along with] four other companies and two steamers – one was the steamer *Planter* that the negroes had run out of Charleston – went up to the city of Bluffton on the mainland. We drove in their pickets from one post to another for about four or five miles. Their pickets were all mounted on horseback. We got one piano and a good deal of fine furniture for the fort. It was all deserted but [for] one house on the upper end of the city. They had the tables all [laid] out for dinner when they saw us coming [so] they left.

We were all very tired as it was a hard day, but we got on our boats and left. We started about twelve o'clock in the night and got back the next night around nine or ten. General Mitchel has sent several black men as scouts to find out the position and strength of the enemy. There are two men here [who have] been here since Saturday and they think that they are going to steal their way into Savannah. There are reinforcements coming and we expect them every day. I believe that we are going to attack the railroad between Charleston and Savannah and destroy the bridges or otherwise we are going to attack Savannah City. They are repairing the boats and putting the guns on them at the present time. At Hilton Head they are making all the preparations. The possibility is that we are going to have two batteries of artillery with us. I am in great hopes that this expedition will not prove a failure as all reports [say that] there is but a small band of Rebels. Down here we don't hear anything from Washington, nor have I heard from you in a long time.

Thomas to Maggie,
Good Bye!

There are deserters coming here every week from Savannah city. They sent out a picket a few days ago. Two of the men and one corporal were to relieve another picket that had been standing for a few days. Well, he got into the boat to steer and the two men were to row. He drew out a nice six-shot revolver and said to the men, "I want to go to Fort Pulaski and you must pull me there. If you say no or won't obey me, I will blow out your brains." They landed here yesterday morning at daylight and he gave up his men, pistol, and himself. He now has his liberty and the two Rebels are kept under a strict guard. They will go to Fort Lafayette. They are Rebels to the backbone, as the man said. The corporal that drove them down here was born in Maine. He is a true Union man. Several weeks ago he was teaching school in the country. They came and took him and 20 of his scholars, all that were able to shoulder a musket.

The Rebels are in a state of starvation. They have had no coffee since July. Their living consists of cornbread and boiled rice only. They are nearly destitute of shoes and clothing. If half is true of what I hear, I believe they can't hold out this winter. I believe Savannah and Charleston will be in our possession in less than 10 days if we have any kind of luck at all.

From your brother till death
Thomas Jones

Fort Pulaski, Georgia
Oct. 27, 1862
Dear Sister Maggie,

I thought [that] I would send you a few lines in this mail to let you know that we are all well. If you remember in my last letter I spoke of Co. B of our regiment going up to Bluffton [and of] the fight they got into. Just as they were leaving, one corporal from Co. B got wounded and he only lived to the next day. Alexander Hyers has been promoted to corporal in his stead. The lieutenant that was with us got wounded in the breast. He is yet alive and the doctor thinks that he will get well. He belongs to the Rhode Island artillery. He was encamped alongside us at Ft. Hamilton and he was with us on James Island. He has been in the fort with us ever since. His men think a great deal of him [as] he is a fine officer.

We found out yesterday evening from a Rebel paper that we killed a major in the 47th Georgia regiment and wounded a general. Fourty privates were killed _____ and this is their own account of it.[24]

> Your Brother Till Death,
> Thomas Jones

Ft. Pulaski, Georgia
November 15, 1862
Dear Sister Maggie,

The Rebels are picking the logs out of the river for their gunboat to run out.[25] She will get a warm reception as at the front tier of the fort is Co. D's Battery. I help man the best gun. It is a rifled cannon.

---

[24] Food shortages in the city of Savannah caused much of the desertion rate and this is a testament to the effectiveness of the Union blockade. Also, the expedition referred to early in the letter was undertaken on October 18 up the May River. The deceased corporal was George Durand.

[25] Pilings were sunk in certain channels to obstruct river traffic.

I think we can use some of the railroad iron. From the battle up in Pocotaligo[26] the Rebels say in their papers that they buried 80 of the 48th along the shore, but there was not a man hurt. There is one report that we killed 90 of the Rebels and among them was the major of the 47th Georgia. The want vengeance on the 48th and they say they will not leave a man of us alive. But it will take a smarter regiment than they have in the Confederate army. The colonel of the 47th NY says, give the 48th and the 47th a raft of logs and they will take Savannah!

Only one man was felled by the enemy. He was killed at Bluffton. The war will soon be over I hope.

You say that you have snow home. I have not seen any snow since I left home.

> At present from your brother till death
> William Jones
> Goodbye!

Letter not headed
December 13, 1862[27]
Friend Maggie,

I have seated myself along the railroad in a little brush house for the purpose of informing you where we are camped. We have laid out doors since we do not have tents and we do the best we can. We started through Washington and marched for five days. We arrived in this place. It is Aquia Creek. We marched to Fredericksburg within four miles and turned and came back. We dropped guards along the railroad. I was left here with a squad of men we had met on the march. A battle commenced on the 11th at Fredericksburg. We

---

[26] Pocotaligo, SC was a strategic point midway between Charleston, South Carolina, and Savannah, Georgia, as it controlled the only railroad linkage between those two cities.

[27] This letter was included in the collection because of its simplistic insights in the life of the Civil War soldier as well as for the surprising lack of military censorship.

can hear the cannon as they discharged. They commenced about daylight and are at it yet. We have just been ordered to put on cartridge boxes and get ready, for Stuart's cavalry [is] making [its] way here. We had the pleasure of seeing 109 Rebel prisoners. They were taken yesterday and were sent to Aquia Creek. Our men are in Fredericksburg and I guess that it is a hard battle by the way the cannon are going. Well, if they come I will do my duty.

I have often heard of forced marches but never experienced them. I cannot give you the particulars, but if you look in the Monmouth Democrat you can see some of our movements. The knapsacks are what kill the soldiers. I thew away very nearly everything I had in order to lighten my load. We don't know how soon we will have to go into the field of battle.

From Your True Friend

J. D. Fogerty

Fort Pulaski, Georgia
December 27, 1862
Dear Sister Maggie,

I soon sit myself down to write you a few lines. Everything is still down here at present and the boys are all well.

I hear Burnside is defeated with the loss of 25,000 men.[28] 25,000 is not much for a general to have some practice. There is no man in the U. S. that will command that army as General W____. If they had sent the 25,000 with General Mitchel when he came here there would be something done.

You say that you go to school. That is very well. You spoke about the vacant desks in the schoolhouse. Some will never be filled again by the same ones that filled it a year ago. I feel I will never fill one

---

[28] William is referring to the Battle of Fredericksburg although his figure is approximately double the number Burnside actually lost. Also note the reference to Gen. Mitchel. He had replaced Hunter on September 16 as overall commander of the Department of the South.

again. Give my love to Hattie and Father and Mother and the rest of my old friends.

Write soon.

From your brother till death, William Jones

Camp D 48 New York Volunteers

Good Bye!

Ft. Pulaski, Georgia

January 10, 1863

Dear Sister Maggie,

I received your kind letter today and was glad to hear from you and from home, from mother and father and Haddie.

Last Thursday and Thursday night I was on guard. A storm commenced. It blew and rained all night. My post was on the ramparts. The first time I went on in the night my cap blew off but in the morning I got my cap. During this time I never thought of home but thought of the damn generals for keeping this war so long. I did not enlist to fight for those black devils. [29]

Never mind $13 a month for fighting for your country. Now we are fighting for blacks and our pay is raised to $16 a month, so you see the difference. They don't pay us what they owe us; now the first of next month there will be six months pay due us.

When you hear of us getting paid of you will see money, for I'm going to send it home and I expect to see a kitchen and a yard fence when I get home. If I ever live to go home. No, no, remember, I mean just what I say.

The British have sent 40 vessels to break the blockade of the South. We have not seen them yet. They had better keep out of old

---

[29] The Emancipation Proclamation went into effect on January 1, 1863. This letter reflects a pervasive mood that arose among Northern Soldiers. Many felt that they had enlisted to preserve the Union, not free the slaves. Thus, President Lincoln's emancipation was ill-received. As for the reference to a British flotilla, this turned out to be mere rumor.

Pulaski. If they come here we will, I am afraid, fill both channels with splinters.

If they come here they will go outside quicker than they came in. There is no fleet that can come and knock down the walls of Pulaski- that is out of the question. So they had better go back and wait. The boys are all well at present and me too. It is raining hard. Give my love to all at home. I may close.

From your brother till death,
William Jones

Fort Pulaski, Georgia
February 18, 1863

As today is a stormy day and I have nothing else to do, I thought I would try and write a little more to you. It will all help to pass away the time. At present, the band is practicing and the officer of the day has just gone through the quarters to see that everything is in good order. There was a flag of truce that went up to Savannah a few days ago. Our steamer took up some ladies and mail. John D. Cottrell was on our steamer and they were together quite a while. John D. had quite a talk with one of the Rebels. They say up in Savannah they can get hardly the least little article, even soap is hardly to be had. There is very much in want of the necessities of life but they say they will hang out to the last minute before they will give up the negro. They say that is all we are fighting for. It is too bad that so many brave men have to sacrifice their lives for the sake of freeing the blacks and after it is accomplished, if it ever is, who is to thank the soldier for what he has suffered and endured since the war commenced? And still the cry is to free the nigger and let the cost be what it may to liberate no less than four million slaves and spread them all over the United States. Times are hard but they would be harder then. A nigger is more respected here now than the soldier is.

The 9th N. J. is at Hilton Head with General Foster. The day after they landed, I hear they killed three niggers, burned several shanties, and raised thunder in general with them a few nights ago.

Here at the fort our Colonel's nigger got shoved into the moat and he liked to get drowned. The are so ignorant and no person can stand them. If a soldier is found doing anything to one he gets punished and the nigger goes free. That's what makes it worse. There is dissatisfaction all through the army, not here alone, as we read in private letters that our boys get from their friends out of the Army of the Potomac. I hear there is a general growl and fault-finding. The men are all discouraged and down-hearted; they feel themselves duped. I will tell you why. The army that is now in the field came out to put down the rebellion. Now they are fighting on a different scale than when the war first started. If they wanted an army to free the slaves I think they would have gotten a very small army. And taking General McClellan from his command, that discouraged the army a good deal. I am afraid they will never get a man as close to Richmond as he did but still, we must hope for the best—but at present everything looks very dark now. I have finished my letter and talked about nothing but the war. I will try and send you a longer letter next time. Let me know all the news. No more at present.

From your dear brother,
Thomas

Fort Pulaski, Georgia
March 3, 1863
My Dear Sister Margaret,

I suppose you are looking for news from the South long before this time. Well, they have been making great preparations at Hilton Head and there have been ironclads over at Wassaw Sound bombarding all day. I suppose it was at the Rebel battery that they have been trying to take so long. There was very heavy cannonading. One or two days ago on the Rebel steamer *Nashville*, that had been up in Savannah these last six months, was laid in with cotton and tried to run the blockade. She made an attempt to get out just before daylight. One of the ironclads spied her and she ran hard aground.

The ironclad fired three shells at her. One struck her midships and blew her up. She was a large ocean steamer and I will bet the Rebels will miss her. This happened at Wassaw Sound four days ago on this river that goes up to the Savannah River. It is the southern entrance to Savannah and the main entrance to the city. It is strongly fortified. The channel is blocked up so it will be a hard job to take it.

It is believed that this is only a feint on Savannah and that the real alert will be on Charleston. We will know in less than a week. I will write as often as I can and give you all the news I can. Give me all the news you can. No more at present but I still remain your brother till death,

Thomas Jones

Letter not headed
March 4, 1863

Our colonel has just arrived here this morning from Wassaw Sound where our ironclads have been bombarding that Rebel battery that I have spoke to you before about. There is a breach in the battery. All night long our boats kept up a steady firing, about a shot a minute, to keep them from repairing it.[30]

It is a very hard battery to take. It is all built of cotton bales, sand bags and logs. It is on the bank of the Ogeechee River and the channel is very narrow so our boats can't move around and fire but they have to anchor right out in front of the battery. There, the Rebels take good range on our boats. I am afraid it will be a very hard job to take Charleston for the shores are lined with batteries. If this battery is taken before this week is out, I will write and let you know. We are all as well as can be. This morning the weather is very fine. We all go on guard as usual. Our duty is very light and thank fortune we are getting along better than most of the regiments.

So Good Bye!

---

[30] The Rebel battery referred to in these letters was probably Ft. McAllister, a relatively small eight-gun earthwork in 1863.

Thomas Jones to Maggie

Letter not headed
March 18, 1863
Dear Friend Maggie,

I will not forget the front. We all may expect a ball. We don't see many of the negroes now as we are out of their world. They don't have much to say to the soldier. I am scared to get knocked down by the musket. Our time is running short. I hope to see a great victory and not a Fredericksburg retreat.

I can't say that I like the soldiers' life. I don't know who would say so. We have been exposed to everything but death itself, but I am willing to shoulder the musket again.

A soldiers' life is a hard one. They are exposed to all of the storms and to hunger and thirst. They are constantly on guard or drill or combat. We stay out on the field three days at a time. We saw the stars when we marched for the Rappahannock. There, four of our boys deserted after the orders of the expected battle were read. They are right now under arrest. John Caud was one and the rest were from Shark River. He also deserted but come back two days after and was court-martialed and fined only one dollar.

Yours with Respect,
John D. Fogerty[31]

---

[31] There are a few letters from John Fogerty in the collection. He knew Maggie, Thomas and William Jones and may have enlisted in the infantry with them. Later, however, he seems to have transferred to the Navy. The battle he referred to was the debacle at Fredericksburg in December of 1862. The ensuing winter camp at Falmouth, Virginia has come to epitomize the depths of morale for the Union Army and John's letter seems to reflect that mood. Also, his reference to seeing "the stars" as he marched to the Rappahannock, may have been the aurora borealis, or Northern Lights, which reportedly lit up the skies that December, even as far south as Virginia.

Ft. Pulaski, Georgia
March 25, 1863
Friend Maggie,

We could not wish for a better place in the summer. This month and the next are the most sickly months. In fact, I believe that the winter and spring months are more sickly here than others for the reason that the casements are damp and cold in the winter and dry and cool in the summer.

I think that you must have meant John H. Bord instead of William Bord that is reported shot, for William Bord has no wife, or at least had none when he left for the war. I received a letter from Janey. She is all well. There is no news of importance. The expedition has not left Hilton Head yet, nor I do know when they intend to leave.

Affairs at Beneomburg

How uncertain the welcome dues of honor fall from the hand that pilots our ironclad ship of state upon the heads of her pugilistic crew. Promotions of various heights have been showered upon the chaps comprising the horse cavalry and it has produced a remarkable change in the appearance of their lines. Stars shine in the sublime splendor of a meteor on the field of carnage. Stars that shine brightest in the darkest hour of battle are often but the smiles of a corporal upon a solitary cracker sack. [Such] are the deluding pictures of life in this brigade. I have often wondered during my hours of solitude when not even a green-eyed monster in the shape of a ten-cent stamp smites my wallet where that serpent of _____ who deceived our parents in the garden keeps himself in these warlike times. But when I see officers kissing the mouth of the bottle, I conclude that our land has taken winter quarters. The weather about this sphere is quite moist. Our camp is full of life and combs are in great demand. We are making formidable preparations for the siege of Spruceville on to that Gibraltar of the foe. When we start, it will be a magnificent spectacle to see us march, which will occur as soon as we leave here.

I remain your friend ever the same
John A. Woodside Co. D
48 NYSV

Camp Hooker, Maryland
March 26
No year cited, but presumably 1863
Esteemed Friend,

I was glad to receive your letter and to hear that you are well. We have had a hard rain and the river is high. The troops are arguing in our camp that some of the thousands of us are on our way to reinforce Rosecrans in Tennessee. It was reported that the Rebel [General] Stuart had crossed the Potomac River and was going to show us battle. The report turned out to be a hoax but we had made preparations to give him a good whipping. There was a regiment going through the other night and the train stopped on the bridge. It being dark and one of the men, thinking that the train was on the ground, jumped off into the river fifty feet [below]. He broke one of his arms. It was reported that the 29th New Jersey passed through on their way to Tennessee. The trains are running all night.

Respectfully Yours,
Nick Hagerman

Not headed & undated
Dear Maggie,

I have nothing of any importance to tell you now but when I come home I can tell you all. I received a letter from John A. W. He is well. William and Thomas were on picket and John D. had just come off and was asleep. The Captain told them that they are going to stay there all summer. They are now drilling and have nothing to do but go bathing. Why don't you write to me more? There have been a great many men who have left these two cities these past two weeks. I shared letters with a Rebel captive and tears were forbidden to flow.[32] But they did and my heart ached for him as I looked on the picture he bore in his hand of his little babe and wife, gone perhaps never to return. Gone because want and starvation stared him in the face in this prosperous city.

Unsigned

Fort Pulaski
April ___, 1863
My Dear Sister Margaret,

Last evening I received a letter from you bearing the date of March 15, 1863. I will now endeavor to answer it. We are all well as I write this morning with the exception of John A. Woodside. He met with an accident yesterday. We were hauling a mortar down to the dock for the Charleston expedition and John evidently got his finger nail taken off. It will lay him up for a few days. The ironclads have all left Hilton Head and there is a troop ship leaving every day, so look for stirring news from that quarter.

I think I will not be here 16 months more. Is it possible that the South can hold out 16 months? It depends if we will have good luck with the Charleston expedition and with Vicksburg.[33] I wish this

---

[32] Note the reference to sharing letters and reading them aloud to a group. This was often done in camp and it served to comfort the lonely soldier who may have not heard from home or could not read his own letters.

[33] April and May of 1863 saw the intensification of Grant's Vicksburg Campaign as his gunboats ran the Rebel batteries positioned along the heights overlooking the Mississippi River. Furthermore, his army circumvented the Vicksburg fortress by marching overland to the west, recrossing the river at Port Gibson, some forty miles down river. With his army on the east bank of the river, he drove inland toward Jackson,

summer would end it for I am tired of the army. The days are tough and lonely. I would rather spend all day working on a farm than be here doing these drills. It's very slavish what they make us do. We don't have bad gruel down here—fresh meat, baked beans, potatoes or stew. I hope you can tell mother I am as great a hand at tea as she ever was. I do not hear anything about coffee and milk. I am so fond of sweet milk that I suppose that when I get home I will drink a gallon of it. I hope the next letter will be as long as possible, for I need something to get me through these cruel days. You must promise to write me back.

This letter was added to the same correspondence

Today I was on fatigue hauling a large cannon down to a battery that the engineers had built alongside the Savannah River. We have a four-gun battery built right close to the channel and if the rams come down from Savannah to run by us and destroy the wooden boats at Hilton Head, we will do what we can to keep them back.

It is now after dark and the boys have commenced to fiddle and dance. They make so much noise that I can't write. It is worse than at school [during] intermission at noon. William and I [were] on guard this morning. Everything in the shape of a vessel has left Hilton Head and gone for Charleston. I expect they are fighting there now. There is a gunboat lying here in front of the fort to assist in keeping the rams from running out.

We have very nice weather here now. Everything slides along with us just as if there was no war going on. We all look for the war

Mississippi, cut the railroad lines to Vicksburg and then drove westward toward the city itself. The siege of Vicksburg consumed the entire month of June and the city fell on July 4, 1863. Factor in the battle of Gettysburg and one can easily argue that the tide of the Civil War had turned during this single week in July 1863.

to end before next fall. General Hunter says [that] he will burn Charleston and sow it with salt. I hope he will.

So, Good Bye! Let me know all the news.
Thomas
Please send paper as it is hard to come by.

Camp Paris
48 Reg't Co. D. U.S. Army
April 29, 1863
Dear Sister Maggie,

Well, I was sick. I got pork and crackers for breakfast and pork and beans for supper. We get crackers and pork and tea. Captain Knowles has gone home on a furlough. Harbison and Lewiston and Carlton all have gone home on furlough for 30 days. Thomas and I send you 40 dollars, each a 20-dollar piece.

Let me know what George S. P. is about. Tell him I say he is a great soldier. All's still along the Savannah River. I guess the U.S. has been in all the fights that there ever will be in Hell. I tell you we have got the greatest General you have ever read of. He will compare our 48th against any regiment in the South. He accepts anyone as regularly as any other. He's had a great deal of pain and illness. He says there are about as few unruly ones as he ever seen.

Sister, you may think this hard of me because he sent some of them to the guard house but still my heart is with yours, after all he is the greatest man I have ever seen. He thinks more of the 48th than they think of him. He took some of the boys' money to keep for them till they want to send it home. Some said that the 48th is going home, but I can't believe it. We drill one hour in the morning. That is all we do till 6 o'clock; at night we have a dress parade. I hope you have not had a hard winter home. I don't know what snow is. It has been so long since I've seen any. The boys are all out at dress parade. I didn't go. There is a rumor in camp today – they say the South has laid down their arms. I guess the 48th will be in New York before the 4th of July.

Tell Haddie I think that she could hardly find that lock of hair that I sent her for it was so short. The weather is awful warm here, but before the hottest of the weather comes we will be home I think.

Calvin Havens has been in the guard house again. He's been in about nine weeks. You need not tell who told you. Nobody likes him at all.

William Jones

Undated, but probably Spring, 1863
Dear Maggie,

One year ago this morning we were lounging out in the Savannah River. It was a cold, drizzly morning. We lay on the steamer all night, no supper nor breakfast in the morning. It is different with us now since we now have many days of hard work and we came off guard often drenched with rain through and through. There have been a good many changes all around. A good many have kissed the dust but still it goes well with us. I am just as well and hearty this morning as I ever was in my life. William is out with a crowd of boys playing a game of baseball. I never saw him look better. He has his health better here than he had at home and all the rest of the boys are the same way. We may thank God for all this, but times may soon change with us. The heat of summer is coming and I think we have been in one place long enough. I know we can't get a better one, but if we could get changed a round a little, it would help to pass away the time.

Goodbye,
from your brother Thomas

Ft. Pulaski, Georgia
June 8, 1863
Part 2nd

I suppose you will all be wondering how William and myself are getting along. As far as quarters and rations, or grub as the soldiers term it, are concerned, the same old cook that cooked for us this time last year, cooks for us yet.

We fare well. Our guard duty and everything is very light and we have an upstairs sort of a place here where we sleep. We sleep on canvas beds; they are nice and cool. Each one has a bed of his own. One on top of the other - four of us here, two on each side – and windows that we can open or shut just as we please. The room is about 12 by 14 feet square.

I don't suppose there is a regiment in the service that has seen nicer times than we have there last six months. And still I don't like it. A soldier's life will never do for me. I wish we had our time served out and we were all home safe and sound. Twice a week we have minstrels to give us music in the bargain, so you see we could not have it any nicer if we wished it.

Unsigned but possibly Thomas Jones

Ft. Pulaski, Georgia
June 18, 1863
My Dear Sister Maggie,

One year ago today our colonel died. A few days later, David Corlies left us. How fast time slides along. Well, for over eight months we haven't lost a man. Everything went along quiet and nice until a few days ago when a young man in our company by the name of Burroghs was taken sick with the fever and he only lived a little over a week. He lays quietly under the sod now and leaves only a sister in New York to mourn his loss. Two weeks ago he was as healthy as any of us and he had sent to New York for an express box. It arrived here after his death. A good many sick men are in the hospital at present and some have been discharged and sent home.

We have just been turned out to receive General Gillmore. He was in Hilton Head. We was a captain in the engineers and was sent out west before he was promoted to what he is now. General Hunter has gone to Washington and that leaves General Gillmore in full command.

You [may] remember me telling you some time ago about some deserters from Savannah reporting that a ram was coming down the river and would try to get outside. Well, we had supposed that it was a hoax as we had been looking for her for so long and she never showed herself. About one or two nights ago she started [out] and the commander was going to capture our wooden gunboat that was at the mouth of the Ogeechee River and then whip our batteries and then go out and steam right up to Charleston and join the [other] rams they had sent up there. They were then going to cut up thunder in general. Well, yesterday morning we were up about daylight, awoken by the report of some three or four heavy guns. We supposed it was as usual – some blockade runner trying to get into Savannah City. Our colonel, some doctors and some of our officers got aboard a little steamer we have here by the name of *Island City* and steamed over to the blockading fleet to see what the matter was. In a short time there arrived here some 18 or 20 Rebel prisoners, [many] with their arms off and their legs full of splinters. Our lieutenant went aboard her and he said that it was a hard sight. The deck was all covered with blood and the [crew] was old gray-haired men and little boys. I don't suppose _____ out of the whole lot will live. They came right on in by our iron-clad which had been sent to a bend in the river the day before. They didn't know that it was our [ship until] we fired. We shot it through and through [especially] the pilot house. We wounded the pilot. Three shells went through her iron plating and burst inside of her. Then she surrendered. Her name was *The Atlanta*. She had on board 160 men and officers and out of this 90 were killed and wounded. The great iron-clad ram that there was so much talk about is in our possession!

No More At Present,
Unsigned

St. Helena Island, SC
June 21, 1863
Dear Parents,

Well, I suppose you have heard of the great Rebel ram in Savannah last Wednesday. The *Atlanta* ran out of Savannah by way of Wassaw Sound. [We took in] five deserters from Savannah who informed us that the ram was going to run out. Commodore DuPont dispatched _____ monitors up there to wait for her. The *Weehawken* engaged her first and knocked out her pilot house. _____ killed one and wounding twelve. Then she ran aground and put up a white flag. [This was] one of the biggest things since the war commenced. She lays in Port Royal [Sound]. I saw her yesterday.

William Jones

St. Helena Island, SC
June 25, 1863
My Dear Sister Margaret,

We have left the fort and are stationed here on St. Helena Island right across the river from Hilton Head. We slept in our new tents for the first time in over a year and we like it first rate. We left nearly all of our things back at the fort; we brought a change of clothing with us and one blanket. There is talk that we are going back to the fort inside of 30 days. We have plenty of room in our tents [as] we only have 141 in them. We used to have 161 men in them.

Conover Emmons has not arrived yet and I have not heard any news. I feel very lonesome as I have not received any letters from home. [I will send you] a letter [describing] how we are getting along in this department and how our forces are advancing on Charleston. [We are doing so] by way of Folly Island.

Your Brother Till Death
Thomas Jones

CHAPTER THREE

1863-64

Charleston, South Carolina, to Olustee, Florida

The Federal bombardment of Ft. Sumter began on April 7, 1863. Seven Union monitors under the command of Rear Admiral Samuel F. DuPont thus initiated a siege lasting until February of 1865. Their failure to take Ft. Sumter in this first assault meant that a Union force had to land on Morris Island and attempt to subdue Batteries Wagner and Gregg. All of this was part of a larger Federal effort to take the city of Charleston, S.C.

The absence of any letters for a full month is easily explained – the 48th New York was very busily engaged in the assault on Battery Wagner that was situated on nearby Morris Island at the entrance to Charleston harbor. The 48th, along with the 6th Connecticut, 3rd New Hampshire, 76th Pennsylvania, and 9th Maine, compositely known as "Strong's Fighting Brigade," charged Battery Wagner on July 18, 1863. The 54th Massachusetts, made famous in the movie *Glory*, also assaulted the fort. Strong's Brigade actually penetrated the outer defenses of Ft. Wagner before being called to retreat from an untenable position. From the regimental history, we can glean something of the horror of the fighting: "The 48th went into that assault with eight companies and nearly five hundred men, and with sixteen officers. The next morning but eighty-six men answered the roll-call. Fifteen of the sixteen officers were killed or wounded. Such mortality was unparalleled in the war."[34] Strong's Brigade suffered over 1,500 casualties in the assault, including General G. C. Strong himself. Hand-to-hand fighting punctuated the charge.

The fort never fell to direct assault but was abandoned, along with Battery Gregg on September 6, 1863. While the 54th Massachusetts lost 272 men, or 42 percent of its force, the 48th New York actually suffered the greatest percentage loss, 57 percent of its compliment or 242 men. These losses were incurred despite a ten-hour preparatory bombardment which had begun at dawn. (S. T. Foster says that the bombardment lasted seven hours and beginning at noon.) The ground assault began about 7:45 p.m. and ended at 1 a.m. Hunkered in "bombproofs," the garrison was as untouched as the fort itself was undamaged. Consisting of sand and palmetto logs, the walls easily withstood the impact of the 9,000 rounds fired by the Union navy offshore. In all, losses to the Confederates totaled only about 174.

Later references in this chapter are to one of the few land battles fought in the state of Florida, the Battle of Olustee or Ocean Pond. The 48th was part of the Federal contingent of 8,000 men under the overall command of Truman Seymour.

President Lincoln believed that the entire state of Florida, lightly defended by militia, could be easily reinstated into the Union by crisp military action. Quincy A. Gillmore, the new Union commander in the Southern Department, concurred. The stalemate at Charleston and the prospects for an easy victory further made the expedition more appealing.

Truman Seymour's brigade left Hilton Head on February 6, 1864 and took Jacksonville, Florida, the next day. His plan was to drive inland toward the Suwannee River, securing the Gulf Central Railroad. On Feb. 20, he met Rebel forces at Olustee, some 35 miles due east and inland. Seymour at once believed the enemy numbers to be superior and his position therefore precarious. He withdrew to Jacksonville to await further orders, supplies and eventual

---

[34] Abraham, J. Palmer, *The History of the Forty-Eighth New York State Volunteers in the War for the Union* (New York: Charles Dilligham, 1885) 162-63.

withdrawal. The expedition was a Union disaster resulting in the loss of some 1,800 men.

This collection opens with one of the final letters written from Ft. Pulaski before the brothers shipped out. The battle of Charleston had already begun. Also included in this segment are two particularly touching letters from John D. Cottrell as he begins to open a romantic interest in Maggie and muses poignantly of a soldier's life, dreams, and fate.

Undated, but probably early June, 1863
Dear Sister Maggie,

We were practicing an hour of battery the other day and the lead flew out of a projectile and wounded a young man in Co. E. The doctor said he will not live.

I am glad to tell you that our monitors are in great numbers and announced fire on Ft. Sumter Tuesday afternoon at 3 p.m. This news came from head quarters and it is looking like they [struck] the magazines in Ft. Sumter. At this time there is so much smoke in the harbor and though the rebels were evacuating Ft. Sumter they could not see for the smoke there is too thick and whenever they fired the smoke would stay.

There is a gun boat staying here to take the ram when she comes down but the ram has no business with Paxson. Lt. Paxson's Battery is the best battery on this fort.

One of our regiment went to the Head and saw Gen. Terry. He asked him if he would let him go to Charleston and see the fight. He said the General would like to have you go but can't. I have been trying to get your regiment to go to my brigade but Gen. Hunter keeps his eye on our regiment more than any other regiment in the army.

The Inspector General, who inspected all the troops of the United States, says he went back to Washington and in his report to Headquarters that the 48th New York is the best regiment in the volunteer army. He said here that our manual of arms he'd never see beat except an old company of regiment at West Point. The troops of this command are all jealous of us except the New York regiments.

Unsigned

Miss Maggie E. Jones
Farmingdale, Monmouth County State of New Jersey
McDougall General Hospital
Fort Schuyler, N.Y.
July 21, 1863
Dear Father,

I was wounded on the 18th of July by a grape shot in my right arm which made it necessary to have it amputated. I left Beaufort on Monday last and arrived here last night at dark. I am getting along very well. My brother came out all right except for a piece of shell which hit him on the ear. There were four out of the company to come through safe. We had 60-odd men and lost all of them in a week. I am not particular about having you come to see me but if you wish to come, go to General Wool's office on Broone Street, N.Y. and get a pass and come over on the Government Boat. I am not in want of anything at present.

I have no more at present. Please write soon and oblige your son,
Thomas Jones[35]
Address McDougall General Hospital, Ft. Schuyler, NY Ward 8,
Section B

---

[35] The handwriting in this letter is different from Thomas's usual script. Since he lost his right arm and would have been unable to write, it was probably dictated to a nurse or an obliging visitor. Thomas would later teach himself to write left-handed.

Off Charleston
July 22, 1863
Morris Island, South Carolina
Dear Parents,

It is with much pleasure that I sit myself down to write you a few lines so you know that we are all well, at least is what is left of us. We have had very hard fighting. We have been under fire since the 9th of this month. But we are fortified so they cannot hurt us much. The other night we took to storm a Rebel battery, but we were repulsed. The 48th has lost 40 men killed and wounded. Thomas is wounded. Patterson and Alec Hires are all that are wounded from around here. I came through safe with but one scratch. Colonel Green was killed; Colonel Barton wounded.

William

Hilton Head, S.C.
July 24, 1863
Dear Parents,

I wrote to you before I left Morris Island to let you know who is wounded and who came out safe from around West Farms. First, Thomas, A. Hires and G. P. Patterson—I have just heard that Alec Hires is dead but I can't tell. I have not seen Thomas since the night of the charge. I never want to see such a slaughter again. We have come back to the Head to recruit up. Thomas is wounded in the arm. You could hardly step without stepping on a dead or wounded [man]. The 48th is all cut to pieces. Thomas [and] C.P. Patterson are all at Beaufort.

Give my best respects to all,
Yours truly,
William Jones

Hilton Head, SC
July 26, 1863
Friend Maggie,

I am sorry to say that Thomas is wounded in the right arm and will likely lose it. He is in the general hospital in Beaufort and doing well. He is in good health and spirits. He may be sent to New York before long. I am not certain, for we cannot get passes to Beaufort from here. I suppose by this time you have heard all about our fight. The night of the 18th our company was on inspection with 14 privates, one corporal, and one lieutenant. George Patterson was wounded by a shell and badly bruised but whether any bones were broken or not I have not heard. We sent a letter to him to find how he is. Alexander Hyers is missing and reported killed. He was wounded badly and may have since died of his wounds. The rest of us who came from West Farms are all well at present. I thought I would let you know about Thomas. Tell Mrs. Jones not to trouble herself for Thomas is well taken care of and will soon be around. Some of the boys who were wounded, whom we thought would die, are walking around nearly as good as ever. All of our officers who were in the fight are killed or wounded except two captains and our adjutant. We will have it easy for a spell; no drills or dress parade. Nothing but fatigue and guard duty. We started for Charleston and what's left of us are bound to go. There are batteries in plain open sight of Fort Sumter and have knocked a few holes in her. Our works are within 600 or 800 yards of the Rebel Fort Wagner which we charged the other night. The are going to fill up our regiment with drafted men. Our lieutenant and one man from each company are going on to New York to get them on the next steamer. I hope the war will soon be over for I don't like to see so many men killed.

We hear that General Rosecrans is in Atlanta, Georgia sixty miles in the rear of Charleston [and] following up on General [Braxton] Bragg.[36]

Yours Respectfully,
John A. Woodside
Co. D, 48 NYSV

Hilton Head, S.C.
July 28, 1863
Dear Parents,

There have been several steamer loads of wounded going north and Thomas is with them. He has had his arm taken off. I have not seen him once before we made the charge but Lieutenant Carlton told me he was right smart. I think A. Hires is dead but I cannot say.

Patterson is in Beaufort in the hospital. He is getting better and as for myself I was taken sick as I told you in my other letter but now I am well and feeling first rate.

I was sorry for Thomas but such are the fortunes of war. It might have been me just as likely as him so there is no use worrying about it. I may get it yet, but I can't tell. But I am a great chap to look out for myself. There were three battles on Morris Island and out of one I came within a hair's breadth of being taken prisoner, but I got away alright, not a scratch. Our captain got shot in the legs. One will have to come off but he has gone North too and they say he will not live. We went in with 16 officers and came out with two. In a few days they sent our regiment away from Morris Island and I am just as well satisfied. There is but a few of us left. We will be recruited up with drafted men. I supposed Fort Sumter is battered down. That is all the news I have. John D. is well.

---

[36] This paragraph is pure rumor. Rosecrans was confronting Bragg, but in Southeastern Tennessee having just taken Chattanooga. His next objective would have been Atlanta, but the September battle of Chickamauga intervened. Even the mileage cited by Woodside is flawed.

Address to Hilton Head. Give my best respects to all around. I may close.

Yours truly,
William Jones

Ft. Pulaski, Georgia
November 21, 1863
Dear Sister,

As for Thomas's things, all I know of is his overcoat and blanket. [I have] both of them and will send them home. I have no chance to go to the Head. You can't get a pass unless it goes to Hilton Head and gets signed and from there to Morris Island [to be] signed by the Commander of the Department and then back to Fort Pulaski.

[Thomas's] dress coat is not worth sending.

They marked us paid for May and June, but this is not so. We [asked] J.M. Tantum to rectify.

Co. D and the Rhode Island company are on guard every two days so you see that we have it pretty hard. The conscripts are not doing duty yet. We received 30 conscripts and they are all Dutchmen. Our camp is not the same company.

William Jones

Ft. Pulaski, Georgia
November 21, 1863
Dear Sister,

The letter you sent me that I received today touched me more than any you have ever sent. As for the things, I have the overcoat and the blanket, too. I have no chance to go to the Head. You can't get a pass unless it goes to Hilton Head and is signed by the Commander of the Department and from there back to Fort Pulaski again. Often all I have is a blanket and overcoat. The dress coat is not worth sending. And a half a blanket, you know you can get them for less up home. Thomas, you need these things as well as I do. What did you have in your knapsack? Was there a pair of pants in which you had altered the pockets? Do you want your revolver or not? Write soon and let me know. And go to Brooklyn and ask if they marked you paid on the payroll. You received no pay when you were at Beaufort, so make them tell you why. For May and June, you were marked paid when Thomas M. White paid you. You did not get paid in Beaufort. F. Sandstrum realized that mistake. This went out of my head or I would have told you before this time. Make no delay for his time is full with recruiting. If he wants to know who told you, tell him I did. And if he wants to know who told me, tell him a spider. And if he wants to know if I know anything about it, tell him I inquired and found out that you had not been paid on the payrolls of May and June. Watch out for what I said. I see that you put several good things in your few lines, but I can't comply with them. I will relate my story since the Paris Island affair. When we came to Hilton Head I had taken sick and you know when I'm that way I can't eat government grub food. I am not all over it yet. What is the matter with me, I can't say. Before we left Augustine I was alright. So you see just how I've been since that affair on Paris Island. I suppose it was being out in the weather so much. I didn't feel any better that night we carried shells from the house along the beach to the battery. I must have hurt myself there and I feel it yet. I am not the same old Bill. Well, I don't spend money foolishly anymore. We are back in Fort Pulaski. I will be saving more than ever before as my term of service is coming to a close. I will try look out for myself in the future. Well, there are no others in the fort but Co. D and a Rhode Island Company.[37] We are on guard duty every day. We have it pretty hard because the conscripts are not doing duty yet.

I suppose we have received thirty conscripts and they are all Dutchmen and campers.[38] It's not the same company it was, but we still command Hilton Head and Fort Pulaski and the island. There is

---

[37] Possibly the 3rd Rhode Island Artillery.

[38] The term "Dutchmen" is a slang reference to German-Americans and some 200,000 served in the Union armies during the war. Together with the Irish-Americans like the Jones brothers, of which some 150,000 served, nearly one out of every four Union soldiers was a first-generation American (Robertson, 29-30).

a rumor of a fleet coming up here to fire on Savannah. Keep that to yourself or you may get me in trouble, for there is a General Order against writing anything home about the movements in the Department. Tell Thomas to write.

Yours truly,
William Jones

Thomas sends his love to one and all. To Maggie, Thomas says he wants to get home and have a real good time eating catfish and something mother cooks good.

Not headed
December 11, 1863
Dear Maggie,

Tommy Amens and John A.W. and all the rest are all well. One of our company died with the fever. He was a very nice-going man. His sisters were the only family he had in the world. He had a good deal of items in camp. He had gold coins and a good many things in his collection.

When he died his books were handed over to George and he collected about 100 and 40 or so dollars. Ten dollars would be put to use in the camp.

Oh, tell father I am glad he raised such a big crop of wheat.

Yours truly, William Jones[39]

---

[39] William Jones' term of enlistment ended on December 21, 1863. He re-enlisted the next day.

Hilton Head Island, SC
January 24, 1864
Friend Maggie,

We are getting along finely here. Our tents are quite comfortable and are all in good health and spirits. I feel sorry every time I think of Thomas, but such things are the fortunes of war. I have escaped safely so far, but do not know what will take place in the next six months. There is an expedition fitting out [and] there are troops coming here every day. It is more than likely we will be part of it. I have seen nothing of the letter sent to William nor of the letter for myself. I have received no letters from Jane for some time. I suppose she has forgotten her old friends. There is no news of importance for there is no active operation going on in this Department. I have not reenlisted although a great many have. Hilton Head is a dull place with nothing to be seen of any consequence. Once and a while we see a lady riding around on horse back. Most of them are elderly ladies so when we see a pretty young lady, we take a good look at her for I do not consider it unmannerly or ungentlemanly to take good looks at a pretty lady. We are having a large theater built in the village of Hilton Head for our amusement and it will be in operation in a few weeks. Tell Thomas that Company D is not what it used to be for they have filled up the regiment with substitutes and conscripts. The are not the same good-natured boys that our last ones were. John Ronk, James Spear, Corporal Aaron Cole are transferred to the invalid corps who are quartered on Saint Helena Island. John Graham, William McCall, Arthur McGuigan, James Huney, John D. Cottrell, Charles McCreaf are our corporals. Corp. Pimm and Harbinson are now sergeants and McDougall is sergeant-of-the-company.

Give my respects to Mr. and Mrs. Jones. I remain your friend.

With Respects, John A. Woodside Co. D 48th Regt.
To Miss Maggie E. Jones
WRITE SOON AND OFTEN

A newspaper clipping found among the letters from this period:

MILITARY

DEPARTURE OF THE FORTY-EIGHTH REGIMENT VOLUNTEERS FOR FORT
SCHUYLER

The veterans of the Forty-eighth regiment volunteers (of Brooklyn), who one month since returned from South Carolina on furlough, left for Fort Schuyler yesterday preparatory to their departure for Jacksonville, Florida, there to rejoin their comrades in arms.

The regiment is under the command of Lieutenant Colonel Strickland. They assembled at Montague Hall, Brooklyn, in New York, where they were ordered to embark for the fort. They were escorted by the Thirteenth regiment National Guard, Colonel J.B. Woodward, preceded by a band of music. Among the officers present were Major General Dutea and staff, General Smith and staff, General Crook's staff, Colonel Dole, of the Fifty-second, and other officers attached to the local militia.

The re-enlisted veterans numbered nearly three hundred men, of which about two hundred reported yesterday before taking up the line of march. Many of the others reported at Montague Hall during the day, and all will doubtless reach the fort in a day or two. The ranks of the regiment will be filled with new recruits from Riker's Island, after which they will embark for their destination.

Palatka, Florida
March 18, 1864
Dear Sister,

Well, on Friday morning we started on the steamer from Fort Schuyler, New York and embarked on land. Then we sailed for Port Royal. We arrived on Wednesday and in the afternoon we embarked on board the steamer *Dictator* [?] and sailed for Florida. We got to Jacksonville and they sent us up the river ten or eleven miles.

Our brigade is here now at Palatka. It is a small village on the St. John's River. We have no tents, but we have little shanties built by hand.

John A. Woodside was slightly wounded. He is alright now. The boys all look like black negroes. We missed the hardest marching and fighting that has ever been done in this department. I sent a good deal of money home and I will be saving more in the next term.

Give my best respects to father, mother, and the little girl with the red hair.

Address Hilton Head
same usual. Yours truly,
William Jones
Good Bye!

Palatka, Florida
March 19, 1864
Friend Maggie,

We just arrived here yesterday. This is a very nice place and I think that we shall stay here for some time. We are but one hundred miles up the St. John's River. There aren't any Rebels around here, only some cavalry about ten miles away. I don't believe that they are fool enough to come down here to get killed. We have got this place arranged so as to keep back a hundred thousand troops, or rather Rebels, and they are well aware of that. We would not stay in enemy country without having good fortifications.

John Woodsides was not wounded very badly, he is on duty again and is well and hearty.

Don't fail to write for it will revive the drooping spirits of a weary soldier.

Your True Friend 'Til Death,
John D. Cottrell

Palatka, Florida
March 27, 1864
My Old Friend Maggie,

It is Sunday today and I could not improve my time better than to spend penning these few lines to one of my old friends...and one that I believe is a true friend, and one that will never forsake a lonely soldier that has always proved true to you and to you only.

Now Maggie, I don't know how to present such things. But since I have returned to this wild country, they all come back to my mind.

Things are very quiet here now and I guess that they will be so for some time to come. The boys are all quite well. My friend T. Brassas was playing a good tune for us last night.

From your affectionate friend 'til death,
John D. Cottrell
I am still the same Jersey Jack!

Palatka, Florida
March 28, 1864
Friend Maggie,

On guard tonight. This a lonely place and for two long hours I must pace to and fro amid the tall old pines fringed with moss and linking vines. Scarcely there smiles a star through the clouds aloft. The ocean breeze is damp and soft that fans my fevered cheeks and brow. On guard tonight, I think of home and the loved ones. This a lonely beat and with a heavy heart and weary feet, I slowly travel forth and back to guard against a night attack.

Oh, yesterday morn, how lightly throbbed full many a heart that death has robbed of its warm pulse. The caskets lie as cold as the winter's starless sky. How sad the thought that another day may find us rushing to the fray and see the close of the morrow's light. We, too, may sleep like those tonight past midnight hour... I long to hear the step of the sentinel, ever dear the sound that vanishes his grief. The welcome tread of the next relief. I hear them come and I can keep my next four hours in the land of sleep. I can dream of home and the loved ones there. May they never know a soldier's care.

From your affectionate friend 'til death,
John D. Cottrell
Please direct to Hilton Head, S.C.
Company D. 48th Regiment N.Y.S.V.

Central Park Hospital
April 24, 1864
My Dear Sister,

Your letter arrived today. I am glad that you are well. You ought to be thankful that you are all so well when there is so much sickness in the neighborhood.

About coming home, they have stopped all furloughs here so if I were to come home I would only have a pass for twenty-four hours. Then I could just stop home for one night. Then if I got delayed and I couldn't return before my pass would be up, they would be very strict here. Some get punished for staying over their pass time. I don't know whether to take my discharge or not. They have raised the soldiers' pay three dollars and a half and that will make all together nineteen and a half dollars each month.

Just let me know if you think I can get a job that will pay me $19 [and] room and board each month. If you do I will be glad to accept it. Just give me your opinion on this subject.

Goodbye from your brother 'til death
Thomas to Maggie
Good bye!!

Gloucester Point, Virginia
10th Army Corps
April 25, 1864
Friend Margaret,

On the morning of the 18th we went to Beaufort and left there the morning of the 20th. We started for Fortress Monroe and arrived there on the morning of the 22nd. We came here the next day and pitched camp. Today finds William and I in our tent using the pen to let our friends know that we are yet on the land and among the living. This is a very pleasant place and I guess that in a short time you will hear of the Army of the Potomac making a move toward Richmond. I think [that] we shall move in the same direction.

I will give you a short history of our trip from Palatka. We left there on the afternoon of the 13th and [went] to Jacksonville, [arriving] there on the morning of the 14th and land[ing] on the 15th. We came down the St. Johns River, but the tide was low and we could not get out. The tide was not high enough until the morning of the 18th, so at six o'clock we cleared the bar and at night arrived at Hilton Head, about _____ o'clock.

John D. Cottrell

Central Park Hospital, NY
April 29, 1864
My Dear Sister,

Your letter arrived and I am glad to hear that all are well. I sent another letter to William yesterday. I have received no answer to my first one yet. He is near Yorktown not far from a place they call Old Point Comfort, so I understand. Write him often as you can. I guess if he had known he was going to leave Florida he wouldn't have sent for his watch. I hope you have not sent it for I believe he would not want to be bothered with it on a march. The Army is receiving large reinforcements and I expect the Army of the Potomac will have a very large battle there before long. There is no news here whatsoever; everything is dull and all eyes are eagerly directed towards the movements of the spring.

From Your Brother, Thomas

Glouster Point, Virginia
Head Quarters 48th Regt.
May 2, 1864
Dear Friend Tom,

I thought I would pen you a few lines thinking you would like to hear from us and about how we are and have been since last February. We are all in good health and hoping you are the same. Tom, we have had some rough times. I suppose you have heard all about the Florida expedition. I was struck twice on the head and wrist breaking the skin a little, nothing serious. Will was reading me your letters last evening. Now, I am very well pleased with your advice. I think I shall practice it for the future. So you think there are a great many boys in the same hospital where you are? I think they ought to be out here giving their comrades a helping hand. Tom, our regiment went into the fight at Olustee with 400 men and left 200 behind them when we fell back to the campground at Burbees Plantation.[40] That was more than half we lost there although a number returned since. A great many were without injury but slightly wounded and fell to the rear. Pete Anderson never re-joined the army till the first day after the fight and he got hit on the chin. The ball raised a black and blue spot about the size of your thumb nail. I suppose that this summer campaign will see more fighting than we have seen before. Well, so be it. It has got to be done and the sooner the better for all hands. We were reviewed by General Butler last Saturday and the review lasted almost all afternoon. We have just received orders to be ready to move at three o'clock.

John A. Woodside

---

[40] Possibly Barber's Plantation.

CHAPTER FOUR

1864

Virginia

Grant's invasion of Virginia was to be the final act in the drama of the Civil War. Beginning with the battle of the Wilderness in May of 1864, the war's most sustained fighting began. In the final tally, it was to be the bloodiest act of an already horrific bloodletting. Besides the Wilderness, there would be the Bloody Angle at Spotsylvania, the frontal assaults at Cold Harbor, and the trench warfare at Petersburg. The end was in sight, but few soldiers in either army were ever sure that they would live to see the final curtain call.

With Grant's army plunging southward toward Richmond all through the spring of 1864, General Robert E. Lee contested him at virtually every major crossroad and river crossing. Inexorably falling back into his defenses at Richmond, Grant actually outfoxed Lee by slipping south of the capital city to assault a lightly defended Petersburg. Located less than 30 miles below Richmond, Petersburg was a vital rail link into which converged the Weldon Railroad, the Southside Railroad, and the Richmond and Petersburg line. Securing the city and cutting these rail links would isolate Lee in Richmond.

Ironically, Petersburg should have been taken much more easily than it was. Ben Butler could have taken the city in early May, but deemed it less than valuable; William F. Smith could have punctured Confederate General P.G.T. Beauregard's thinly held trenches in mid-June but grew timid after initial successes against the outskirting trench lines of the city. Some accounts say that his memories of Cold Harbor were too vivid.

Once Lee realized the Union design, he hurried troops southward along the very same rail lines that should have earlier fallen into Federal hands. Beefing up the city's defenses, Grant could only opt for a siege. The siege was to last nine months—292 days—and in many ways it was to be the most vivid harbinger of modern war that this conflict was to raise.

Not only would the trench fighting and urban destruction which characterized the Petersburg siege become commonplace in twentieth century warfare, but also Grant's approach to attritional tactics would be replicated, albeit on a larger scale, in the Second World War by Dwight D. Eisenhower. With superior manpower and supplies, Grant sought to extend his trench lines around Petersburg, further hooking them to the west. Not only would this cut the Southside and Weldon Railroads, but it would also force Lee to counter it with further extensions of his own lines thereby thinning out the manpower resources needed to man the works. Eisenhower's "broad front" strategy in World War II would be reminiscent of this. Thin out the enemy lines and eventually a breakthrough can be achieved.

After the initial assaults on redoubts number five and eight which fell to Union troops, the southern approaches to Petersburg were in Union hands. Grant soon arrived with the main body of the Union army and he set about building a supply depot at City Point on the James River. This port became the logistical nerve center for the Union siege operation and even a railroad was built directly to the trench lines.

As Grant inched his lines westward, Lee was forced to defend a thirty-five mile front extending from Richmond to a point south and west of Petersburg. This front would eventually become seventy miles long by the spring of 1865. Whereas Grant was able to put

109,000 men on the field, Lee was able to counter with only 59,000. On a purely statistical basis, this would graphically translate to Lee's army with a man every yard, but Grant's men could be arrayed shoulder-to-shoulder for the entire length of the line. Literally something, somewhere, was bound to give.

The siege of Petersburg involved six major battles and eleven engagements including the famous Crater, the storming of Forts Mahone, Gregg, and Stedman, and the battles of Hatcher's Run and Globe Tavern, plus forty-four skirmishes.[41] The eventual outcome would see the battles of Five Forks, Saylor's Creek, and a surrender at Appomottax Court House.

In all, Union forces suffered 42,000 casualties against a Confederate loss of 28,000. Factor in the 50,000 casualties Grant's army took in just one month of fighting when he first began his invasion of Virginia and one can begin to realize the grim costs of modern war.

As for the 48th New York, the regiment was sent northward on April 23, 1864 to join General Ben Butler's Army of the James. This contingent was to slice upward toward Richmond by moving up the James River while General George G. Meade's Army of the Potomac, with Grant in their midst, would press Lee's Army of Northern Virginia from the north. William Jones would describe actions related to Cold Harbor, Deep Bottom, Hatcher's Run, Strawberry Plains, and Petersburg itself. Butler's army would essentially fail in its mission by entrenching along a loop in the James called Bermuda Hundred and Dutch Gap. He would, in effect, bottle himself up. As a teamster, it may be assumed that William Jones found himself making contact with elements of both armies once the siege lines began to form around Petersburg.

The 48th New York was in the Petersburg trenches when the famous Battle of the Crater took place. The date was July 29, 1864 and the project was the brainchild of the 48th Pennsylvania, a regiment made up largely of coal miners' sons. They dug a 511-foot tunnel under the Confederate lines and then placed 320 kegs of

---

[41] Frances H. Kennedy, editor, *The Civil War Battlefield Guide* (Boston: Houghton Mifflin, 1990) 253.

powder totaling four tons. The ensuing explosion decimated a South Carolina regiment and opened not only a 170-foot crater three stories deep, but also a 300-yard gap in the Rebel lines. From there, the expedition went awry. Palmer's regimental history offers these descriptions and insights:

> Suddenly the very earth on which we stood seemed to tremble; the fire had reached the magazines, and, with a mighty shock, followed by a rumbling like that of thunder, the whole Confederate fort in our front was lifted into the air. A dense mass of smoke covered it, and flying fragments flew everywhere. The entire work was demolished, and its garrison of three hundred men buried in its ruins. In a moment, as the smoke cleared away, we saw a vast crater where the fortification had been...
>
> Instantly the Federal guns opened a heavy cannonade and bombardment for miles all along our lines. The dismayed Confederates only made a feeble response. The way was open to us—the enemy was at our mercy.
>
> And now occurred the most lamentable failure and the most inexcusable of the whole war. Ledlie's division, which its commander should have led in person straight through the crater and on to the crest, went no further than the site of the ruined fort. The divisions of Potter and Wilcox followed him, but their way was blocked by Ledlie's halted columns... It was the old blunder of Fort Wagner repeated at Petersburg: not that the colored soldiers did not come forward bravely enough; but they were not in position at the proper moment, and the delay was fatal. The enemy were in a state of panic; aroused from their sleep in the trenches by the terrible explosion, it was a long time before the officers succeeded in rallying them. The mine had exploded at fifteen minutes before five; it was half-past seven when Ferrero's colored division advanced to the breach....
>
> A terrible fight now ensued among the struggling and disorganized masses of men in and about the crater: some of them forced their way into the ditch of the gorge-line, where they fought with the enemy hand to hand; others crept along the

glacis of the exterior line and climbed over the parapet into the main trench. The rebels fought behind their traverses. But it was useless: the priceless moments had been wasted. Our losses were estimated at 4,400; the Confederate losses at not more than a thousand, including those who had been blown up with the fort.[42]

A combination of poor timing, officers' ineptitude, and drunkenness, and poor tactical leadership by the Union General Burnside sealed the fate of the battle. The Federals withdrew back to their trench lines with no gain and a protraction of the Petersburg siege for another eight months. The 48th New York lost 29 men in the assault and was given a two-week respite at Bermuda Hundred.

General Benjamin Butler's Army of the James had landed at a strategically located bend in the James River on May 5-6. He immediately set about entrenching across the four-mile neck of land that runs from Farrar's Island to Port Walthall. With the looping river securing his flanks, Bermuda Hundred lay behind him. Butler was therefore in a position to plunge southward to Petersburg or drive north toward Richmond, each point being less than twenty miles away. Furthermore, he could drive inland to cut the Petersburg-Richmond railroad or secure a base of operations at nearby City Point. All were within Ben Butler's grasp.

He tried to do it all. Indecisively probing in all three directions, his troops burned bridges and tore up railroad tracks. Between May 7 and 10, his forays worked their way toward Petersburg while regiments on loan from Quincy Gillmore sliced westward to take Chester Station. Not believing Petersburg to be of any significance, he withdrew to Bermuda Hundred and then ordered northward movements toward Drewry's Bluff on May 12-15.

Again withdrawing amid much infighting within his officer staff, Butler's 30,000-man force fell back to Bermuda Hundred to wait further orders and coordination with Grant. One fellow officer wryly

---

[42] Abraham, J. Palmer, *The History of the Forty-Eighth New York State Volunteers in the War for the Union* (New York: Charles Dilligham, 1885) 162-63.

noted that despite his strategically valuable location, Butler's army was "corked" in the great bend in the James.[43] Moreover, had Butler been more aggressive toward Petersburg, the war may have ended sooner.

More of John D. Cottrell's letters are included in this chapter. I find them eloquent and poignant expressions of the mood of the fighting man in the waning months of the war. Some items to look for in this chapter include William's graphic letter of July 5, the soldier's feelings about the Election of 1864, a touching letter from one of Maggie's friends who lost a close relative in the war and the letters of John A. Woodside containing interesting information and observations on events in the Petersburg trench warfare. An interesting poem from John D. Fogerty of the 29th New York is also included. These additional letters, while not from her brothers, must have been treasured by Maggie as she thought it appropriate to keep them with those from her family.

Near Petersburg, Virginia
May 11, 1864
Dear Parents,

Our arms are victorious in this part. We had a pretty hard fight the other day in which our brigade behaved very well. We made a charge on the Rebs [along] the railroad and drove them back. We [then] tore up the track.[44] Our regiment lost 60 men killed, wounded and missing. We have had a fight every day since we came here, but we have only been in one. There was a hard fight yesterday in which we were sent to the front but the enemy was repulsed with

---

[43] Shelby Foote, *The Civil War: A Narrative History* (New York: Random House, 1974) 2:251-264.

[44] It is a curiosity as to which railroad was referred to here. William may have been citing a probing attack toward the Richmond-Petersburg line in the area of Chester Courthouse or south of Petersburg along the Norfolk & Petersburg Railroad.

a heavy loss. They charged our light artillery. We did not get a chance at them. Thank God I have come [through] alright so far. You wanted to know if I ever thought of home. Well, perhaps I do think too much [of home].

You will please excuse this poor writing and dirty paper for I am on duty.

From Your Dutiful Son,
William Jones

May 19, 1864

It has been some time since I wrote to you and I suppose that you are aware of the reason it has been so long. I am now in this hospital with a nick in the skull, but by good luck it is not very bad. I think that if I have good luck I shall soon get smart. I am wounded in the head and shoulder. The rest of the boys are all right. I was wounded last Monday, about nine o'clock. William was there and stood it all and came back sound, but poor Thomas Brassas—was killed dead in the first round. He was shot through the breast with three balls and died in less than a minute. It was a hard fight, but I cant' give you a detail of the battle this time for my arm is too weak to write. The regiment is back at Bermuda Hundred near City Point. The fight was near Fort Darling.[45] The Rebels are getting whipped in every fight

---

[45] Fort Darling was on the James River atop a ninety-foot high cliff known as Drewry's Bluff. It was the site of two attacks during the Civil War. The first occurred in May 15, 1862 as a Union naval squadron, which included the famous *USS Monitor* attempted to navigate the bend in the James, bombarding Ft. Darling and steam past and on into Richmond just seven miles away. The small garrison and their three Coumbiad seacoast guns foiled the attack. Two years later, on May 9, 1864 Ben Butler's Army of the James attempted to take the fort from the landward side. While some Union troops gained the fort's outer perimeters, their attack was called off

and are driven back with heavy losses. I shan't write much this time for I don't believe that you can read it.

Unsigned but probably J.D. Cottrell

Friday the 20th, 1864
Perhaps May

There is good news here but I can't tell you all at present. General Sigel has captured 15 thousand prisoners yesterday, and they arrived here this morning, or at least a good portion of them. There were about 40 thousand here before, so I think that if the Rebels keep falling into our hands, there won't be any of them to fight after a while. I suppose that you will see an account of the fight before you get this letter. I shall send you a little keepsake in this letter which was mailed by a Rebel prisoner. The mail comes every day and we get the papers every day. This is a splendid place for the wounded to be and the best of care is taken of them.[46]

From your affectionate friend,
John Cottrell
Hammond General Hospital
Point Lookout, Maryland

---

and the fort held once again. It is still there for modern visitors to enjoy although only a relatively small portion of the original fort remains. The commanding view of the James is still impressive, however.

[46] This is an oddly dated letter since the record of any significant victory by Franz Sigel in 1864 is lacking. In the spring of that year he commanded Federal troops in the Shenandoah Valley. His forces were defeated in the Battle of New Market in May, 1864 amid which occurred the famous charge of the Virginia Military Institute (VMI) cadets.

Chester, Virginia
May 21, 1864

We have been under _____ every day since the 7th of May. Two nights ago I was under a galling fire in the afternoon. Previously the Rebs came in on us before we saw them. We were at the front in the rifle pits. There was only about _____ of our company on the left, and they came in on us. We repulsed them handsomely, but the regiment turned a left flank fire on them and drew back to the skirmish line. Our camp lost one killed and one wounded. When you write to Thomas, tell him that Enoch Allen got killed.[47] He was making calculations on getting home soon. He would not reenlist. The enemy has driven us inside of our entrenchment and are building batteries under our nose, but there is a strong force of them. There is a trap for them if they charge on our ranks. We open only one battery on them, but there are about 100 guns if they charge on us. You will see a great slaughter. I close for I am greatly in need of some sleep. I need not speak about Thomas Brasass. He fell on Monday last. I don't know how soon it will become my turn. Calvin Havens is here with me tonight and, he wishes to be remembered to you. All the drums are beating. I will bid you good night.

From Your Affectionate Son,
William Jones

Chesterfield Co., Virginia
May 26, 1864
Dear Parents,

A day ago the regiment, or rather the brigade, left for some place but I don't know where. The sick men were left behind and they are out of the regiment. We moved west toward the fortifications but

---

[47] The regimental history of the 48th New York states that Enoch Allen was killed in action near Hatcher's Run, Virginia on May 19, 1864.

attacked nothing. Again, I can't tell you my address. The sick from all the regiments are here and they have nothing to do but to go out and work. In case of an attack and if I don't get your letters, they will be taken care of by the company until I return. I will write to you three times a week. I am not in danger but I am unwell and unable to march so the doctor told me to stay behind. I thought to myself that I had gone through enough since I was recruited. I will write to Thomas and Janie today and if a letter comes I will let you know.

Wm. Jones

Central Park Hospital
May 29, 1864
My Dear Sister,

Your letter arrived with William's inside of it. I am glad [that] things are as well as they are and no worse all around. They have had a very hard time of it down here according to all accounts. I am very glad that William has gotten along so well. There are some very hard looking cases which have come here the past few days. One [member] of our regiment [arrived] here last evening bleeding to death. One of his arteries had burst. He was badly wounded in the breast.

I had a letter from William [which was] later than yours. I hope you write to him often. Send him stamps and envelopes already directed and small pieces of paper inside [as] there is no sutler with him.

I send you my love hoping to hear from you soon.
Thos. Jones

Hammond General Hospital
Ward No. 15
Point Lookout, Maryland
June 5, 1864
My Dear Friend Maggie,

At present, times are very still. I had a letter from William the other day and he was alright then. You said in your last letter that I must tell you who saw Thomas Brassas die and who was with him. I saw the fellow who was with him when he died. He belonged to his company and that is all that I know about it.

This same fellow told me of his death when I was coming from the field and he said that Thomas was trying to rally the company together after they broke and fell back. This is when he was shot.

I trust this cruel war will soon be brought to a close and the Rebels made to lay down their arms and come in and give up. I want to hear of that very badly and very soon.

From you ever true and affectionate friend,

John D. Cottrell
to his friend Maggie

Central Park Hospital
June 7, 1864
My Dear Sister,

I feel very discouraged today. I see in yesterday's paper that Barton's brigade has left the 10th Corps and gone with General Smith to the 18th Corps, Army of the Potomac to reinforce General Grant. I see they have had a very heavy engagement last Friday and our colonel got wounded [along with] a great many men. I don't see any names of the boys I know on the list of killed and wounded. I had a letter from John D. Cottrell a few days ago and he says [that] he is getting better very fast. He had a very severe fever. The 18th Corps has left _____ department before the _____th of May, but I don't see how our brigade and regiment left [with them]. But they are in the

Army of the Potomac now and I am very sorry for I know [that] there are not many of our old men left now.

[Please] excuse this poor writing.

Thomas Jones to his loving sister Maggie

Hammond General Hospital
Ward No. 15
Point Lookout, Maryland
June 8, 1864
My Dear Friend Maggie,

Maggie, I believe that you said I must let you know about William and how he was whenever I could. Well Maggie, I got a letter from him the other day that was mailed the 30th. He was alright then. The regiment was laying still and just waiting for the Rebels to come and attack them. You said in your letter that you saw in the papers about Butler's army having a fight on Friday and you wondered if the 48th was engaged. They were, but they were just getting released from picket duty. They had been out on picket for 24 hours and it was just after getting off when the Rebels came. Our company lost two men, one killed and one wounded. William tells me that little H. Smith and Conover Emmons have returned and are now on duty.

Your affectionate friend,
John Cottrell

Brooklyn
June 12, 1864
Dear Thomas,

Brother, I was very glad to receive your letter yesterday. It was of great satisfaction to hear from William. I was afraid he was in that battle at Cold Harbor. I see that Col. Barton was wounded.[48] The bullet struck his watch and pierced down his leg. He was suffering very severely. I was glad to know from your letter that he had remained with Gilmore. I sent him an envelope filled with paper last week and again last Monday. I hope he will get them soon, for [he] told me that he had to borrow paper and could scarcely get it.

Thomas, I wish you would tell me what time you expect to be discharged and how long you will be there. I shall try to come up there and if it is a nice day you may look for me. Get a pass if you can. I will let you know before Saturday if I can come.

Goodbye,
Your Loving Sister Janie

Letter not headed
For the Soldiers of the Potomac
Air Annie _____ le[49]

1. Down white Potomac waters,
'Neath the sunbeams' smile,
Lay a soldier meek and dying.
In delirium wild,
Through his vision, the raging fever
Wild and swift did roam,
And the soldier's brain was wandering
'Mid sweet scenes of home.
Chorus! Fond Mother, dear Father,
To the soldier, come.

---

[48] The regimental history of the 48th New York notes that besides the wounding of Col. Barton, the regimental flag was lost in the assault and that Color-Sergeant William H. Porch was killed. Also noted is the fact that among the Rebel soldiers captured was a female officer.

[49] Possibly "Annie of the Vale"

For his brain is wandering
'Mid sweet scenes of home.
2. On his ear there fell the chiming
Of the old church bell;
Came his mother's tones so holy
That he loved so well.
Hear the murmur of the brooklet
In the quiet dell.
Scenes of sport in joyous childhood
O'er him cast their spell.
Chorus!   Fond sister, dear brother,
Greet the soldier now.
And he feels his mother's kisses
On his aching brow.
3. Farewell, Mother, I am gone
To my home of joy.
Place my head upon your bosom;
Kiss your darling boy.
Lay my form within the churchyard
Where I loved to stray,
'Neath the old church wherein I held _____
First I learned to pray.
Chorus! Fond Mother, dear Father,
To the soldier, come.
For his brain was wildly wandering
'Mid sweet scenes of home.
4. Bid my Mary, cease her weeping
When forever I am gone.
Bid her o'er my grave not murmur sadly and forlorn.
Slowly the soldier's eyes were closing
Faintly come his breath, with a murmur,
'Twas but Mary slept the ____ of death.
Chorus! Weep, comrades, for the soldier
Who hath left your band.
Make his grave beneath the willow

In the southern land.

-John Fogerty
Hammond General Hospital
Ward No. 15

Point Lookout, Maryland
June 14, 1864
My Old Friend Thomas,

You will please excuse me for not penning you a few lines before this.

I hope that I shall be all right again in a short time. I am of the same opinion as you are in regards to the draft. I hope that the draft, if there is one, won't miss so many of the West Farms and Turkey [Swamp] boys, as it did before, for I can tell you , my old soldier friend, that it would do me good to see those damned ____ brought out and shoved to the front. It is a pretty big sacrifice for one to make but I should like for all of those lads who have been laying around home all of this time whilst you and me and many others have been out and undergone all the hardships of a soldier's life- and all of that time they are laying back! I see in this morning's paper that Hunter and Sherman have been licking the Rebs again pretty badly. He has captured about 1500 prisoners and 15,000 stands of arms, nine pieces of artillery together with mass quantities of supplies. The body of the Rebel General W.E. Johnson was found on the battlefield so there is another smart Rebel General. You and I wish they were all brought to either the same end or give up, but I can tell you that the Rebels do fight with a great desperation.

I can tell you that on the 16th when I was wounded, the Rebels did fight. In all they charged four times and were repulsed every time and yet still they came on. I was wounded in the fourth charge. They made us all hold our fire till they came very close and then we gave it to them with all of our might. Their columns could not stand the fire of our men. They were in the woods and our men laid just at the edge of the woods behind old logs and rails. We waited until they came within twenty yards before we rose and poured it into them. Now my sheet is full, so I shall close.

John D. Cottrell

Davids Island Hospital
New York Harbor
Undated, but probably June, 1864
My Dear Sister,

I am glad that I have this chance to write you these few lines to let you know that I got here safely. I don't know what will be done with me yet. I came up to Brooklyn with Lieutenant Tantum and we talked over old times till after 12 o'clock at night. We expected a steamer in from Hilton Head with our regiment on board, and if William had come as was expected, I should have gone right straight home again, but we were disappointed when we got up here. We heard they had been seen marching up Broadway, but it was then too late for me. I would like to see the boys first rate, but I don't believe I can see them now, so if William is not home yet you may look for a surprise. This hospital is a nicer looking than Fort Schuyler was.

If William comes home, tell him not to let them Copperheads around there guile him out of too much of his money.

A friend was released this morning out of the guard house, and about 20 minutes later he was put in again.

Yours truly,
Thomas Jones

Writing on my canteen
June 18 [?], 1863
Dear Brother,

I was out on picket before we got relieved. The rest of the regiment went to Petersburg but we stayed out here. Even last night there were enough men left in camp to relieve four companies. We lay [along] the Appomattox River and our mail had come. I received $5 in one letter and another one with blank [writing] paper. I am very grateful. I got one from Maggie with two dollars in it, but it is state money and I had to send it back again. I will close, we will all be relieved soon and go to our trenches at Petersburg.

I will close.
From your Brother William

Central Park Hospital
Friday, June 24, 1864
My Dear Sister,

Your letter has arrived alright and I am very glad to learn that you are all well. I was pleased to learn that William was well and in such good spirits. You told me that you had written to him so I concluded I would just wait a few days before I would write to him, thinking that he might soon decide what he was going to do and where he would settle down in some steady place where he would be certain of getting his letters. I hope he may go in the navy when his regiment is discharged. It will be just the same as if he had never left it and if he lives to come out of it, he won't have his health broken down like a good many have had in the army. I think that when I get my discharge I will have money enough to get a good horse besides paying for my arm.

From your Brother,
Thomas Jones

Petersburg, Virginia
June 28, 1864
Letter not addressed

Writing on my canteen. Six days ago we went on picket duty and before we got relieved the rest of the regiment went to Petersburg.

Last night there were enough men in camp to relieve four companies so they could go wash their clothes and have 24 hours off guard. I will close. We will all be relieved tonight and go to join our regiment at Petersburg.

From your Brother,
William Jones

Head Quarters Army of the Potomac
Near Petersburg, Virginia
July 5, 1864
Friend Janie,

I received your ever welcome letter. This is the first opportunity I have had to answer. We are laying in the rifle pits in the front of Petersburg. The Rebs shell us now and then but they do not kill or wound a great many. They have been throwing them over us today and have hurt none of us. They kept us awake all night on the 3 of July by throwing shell and solid shot into the mortar battery where we were stationed, but they hurt none of us. We watch them closely and when they go over us, we lie back and laugh at them. We can see the church spires in the city and we can see the houses plainly, too. We have not taken the city yet and it will be some time before we do get it. The weather is very warm here. A number of men get sun stroke on account of the heat. When our mortar battery opened fire last night we blew one of the Rebs out of his trench and left him laying on the [parapet] burning. He was blown 20 feet in the air. His comrades tried to get him in the trench again but our sharp shooters would fire at them every time they showed themselves. So they could not get him till after dark. I don't understand what is the matter with you. At home you seem discouraged and downhearted while we are in the best of spirits laughing and joking as if there is nothing going on. We get little rest and little to eat and yet the men are not discouraged. I think we will rest here till the better part of August or the first of September and then commence another campaign [with] the full company. William is well and hearty. J. D.

Cottrell is getting along finely. I also received a letter from Maggie. She seemed somewhat down-hearted. We will come out alright. I hope for the best. There is but one division of our boys here. The others are at Bermuda Hundred and Deep Bottom. We have had two killed since we came here. Sergeant John H. Graham,[50] killed on June 30th, and George W. Richman on July 1st – both by sharpshooters. I hear that Peter Brown has been taken. I do not know where the 14th NJ is now. The last time I saw them they were at Cold Harbor.[51] I saw George Mariner and Russell Hampton. That was all. I did not go to their regiment for I had no time. You must excuse me for delaying so long in answering your letter but I have taken the first quiet opportunity that I have had. There are a few tomato plants growing here and it is fun to see some of the boys putting soil for potatoes to take root.

With best wishes for your welfare and happiness I close.
I remain as ever your friend the same till death,
John A. Woodside

July 8, 1864
Mr. Thomas Jones
Central Park, New York
From his loving Sister Maggie
Dear Brother,

Why do you not write? I have waited now all this week and last for an answer for my last letter, but waited in vain. Received a letter

---

[50] According to the regimental history, John Graham was killed on June 29, "...while trying to run to the rifle pits with some coffee for the men...' William reflects on this episode in a touching letter dated June 30, 1865.

[51] The 14th New Jersey was stationed along the Monocacy River in Maryland and was about to engage Confederate General Jubal Early in the fight of its life on July 9, 1864.

from William yesterday. He is well and yet is at Bermuda Hundred. The division has gone to Petersburg. They are left behind.

There has been another draft here. Harber Woolley is one of the unfortunates. James Lanning, Dennis Wilson, Louis Johnson's son Poe [also] fare among the unfortunates, [as does] John Burden. Joel Brown is very ill ____ his father's name is not among the prisoners. They fear he [has been] killed.

Goodbye
From Maggie

Brooklyn
July 10, 1864
Dear Sister,

I am going to see Thomas before I go home. I got a letter from him last night. He is well but he has not been to see me yet. I think he never intends to come. Maggie, you have heard before this that George Richman was killed by a sharp-shooter. Shot through the head and died instantly, poor fellow. Another one of his comrades was killed.

Now he is all alone, poor fellow. I expect one of these days to hear that he has fallen, too. May God take care of him.

From your loving sister,
Janie

The news has come since I had stopped writing that the greatest part of Lee's army is in Baltimore.[52]

---

[52] Janie is reporting a rumor. In July of 1864, Confederate General Jubal Early did make a serious attempt on the outskirts of Washington, D.C. in an effort to draw Federal forces out of the Shenandoah Valley and from the Petersburg trenches (General U.S. Grant had reinforced his besieging army with men taken from the forts surrounding Washington). Confronting Early's force of about 14,000 was a piecemeal contingent of militia and

Central Park Hospital
July 15, 1864
My Dear Sister,

We have a good deal of fun here. You ought to see the one-armed men and one-legged men playing ball together. We try to engage ourselves here as best we can.

I received a letter this morning from William. He is well and hearty, yet it was written on the 10th of this month. He said that they were in the rifle pits front of Petersburg. No bed but the sand, and that they were as jolly as you please. He says that he and the lieutenant, that is Lieutenant Tantum, had a few of what he calls dry works nearly every evening before they go to bed, then they lay down on the land for the night. I think that he and the officers and men get along very well. He says that he thinks that Lieutenant Tantum will sign the paper for him to go in the navy if the Colonel and General would only agree with it, but he thinks that he will wait now until this campaign is over or until John D. comes back to the company. He says that there has no one been killed or wounded in Co. D. since he last wrote.

No more at present, but with my love to you all, I close.
Thomas Jones

---

hastily thrown-together regiments, numbering about 6500. They were guarding two strategic bridges over the Monocacy River near Frederick, Maryland. They were commanded by Union general Lew Wallace who would later earn fame as the author of the novel *Ben-Hur*. Among his troops was the 14th New Jersey. The two forces clashed on July 9, 1864. Despite the loss of nearly a third of his forces and the field itself, Wallace's men had bought time for reinforcements to arrive in the Washington forts and Early's raid was turned back.

Petersburg, Virginia
July 16, 1864
Dear Sister,

Things are about as usual—only cannoning and sharpshooting are carried on at any great extent, but our casualties are small. I think we are a going to have to make a forward movement before long around here. I tell you they have heavy entrenchments in our front. If we have to charge I will try to look out for myself if I can. We have not lost anymore in our corps since I last wrote. I have some letters on the way for you now.

In regard to those men that were drafted, I am very sorry for Lizzy Midere and Mr. Woolley. He is [a] copperhead anyway.[53] I imagined I just saw Johnny in a rifle pit nearby. He had to keep shooting through a porthole. You dare not stick up your head, but I would leap up and laugh.

I think old Lee is a playing a game of seven-up with our generals at Washington. At the present, I am satisfied with anything.

Goodbye,
William Jones

Before Petersburg,
July 17, 1864
Dear Sister,

I was very happy to receive your letter this morning. I had given up all hopes of getting into the Navy but since you have taken so much trouble I will try again – in this letter you will find a note. Please hand it to Dr. Strickland. I forgot to tell him that my officers are all willing for me to go if I can. Tell him all my reasons are in there except for the cause that my comrades have all been stricken

---

[53] An anti-war Democrat, the most vocal of which was Ohio Congressman Clement L. Vallandigham who was later exiled from the United States.

by the deadly fire of the enemy. I will not detain you with a long letter. I will just say I hope we will not be in so bad a place as we were one year ago tomorrow evening, although we are fully as close to the enemy now as we were then.

Believe me still
Your affectionate brother
William Jones

Give my respect to Father, Mother and Haddie and have a portion for yourself.

Home
July 22, 1864
Dear Brother,

Have you heard that D. T. Cottrell's son, Willie, was killed in that last battle? Cornelius Barkalow was wounded, Captain Cornine also; D.C. Patterson is back with his regiment again. Well, Thomas when shall we look for you to come home? When you expect your discharge, write us a long letter.

From your affectionate sister,
Maggie

From the Field as Usual
Before Petersburg
July 22, 1864
Dear Sister,

The siege of the city is progressing [nicely]. Last night I stood and saw a fine sight. There was an artillery duel and our mortars and siege pieces were throwing shell [which] is a pretty thing to see in the night going through the air. Our batteries opened up and the Johnnies _____ half to death.

I think Uncle Abe is going to open their eyes. [We may have] 500,000 men in the field by September. I think he is going to kill all he can. I hope that won't be long before we get out.

Maggie, in regards to that [business of] getting in the navy, I have written to Dr. Strickland by way of Mary Jane and I hope [that] he will do all he can.

I have been pretty sick for two days.[54] I was sent to the general hospital and then to the convalescent _____. I have seen too many men turned out dead every morning. It scared Bill half to death, so I picked up and traveled [back] to the regiment. I am better now and I hope to be [so] until the war is over for there [are] 500,000 men who will do the same thing.

[If] Sherman down in Georgia is victorious...we can't do anything until we get more men and then I think "Charge" will be the order. Then look out for your heads.

Maggie, I will close. Give my respects to all. Tell mother to put a straight face on Haddie and send me her picture.

William Jones

Hammond General Hospital
Ward No. 15
Pt. Lookout, Maryland
July 24, 1864
My Friend Maggie,

I hope that they may [soon be] lucky in bringing the north and the south to some kind of reasonable terms. Just cast an eye over the battlefields and see how many, [from] both north and south, have

---

54 According to post-war records, William spent the period of July 19-21 in a hospital at Broadway Landing, Point of Rocks, Virginia. In 1882 his oldest daughter Frances tried to file for her father's pension based on his disabilities suffered during the war. William died about this time, but the exact date is unknown. His family did receive his pension.

found their graves and to think how many more it will take to close this [out] by fighting. If it is not ended in this Fall's campaign, it will never end. Now look back at this call of Old Abraham for five hundred thousand. It is going to drain the north petty well. I had better close for it is evening and tomorrow is the Sabbath.

John D. Cottrell

Central Park Hospital
July 24, 1864
My Dear Sister Maggie,

This hospital is situated in a very pleasant place opposite the city of Harlem. We can see the railroad cars pass along very often so if William thinks of coming up here [we] can show him what car to take. There is none in this hospital but cripples and men with rheumatism. In one ward there is nearly a hundred men with one leg off. I like this hospital first rate. I have nothing to do but eat and sleep.

Love to you all,
Thomas Jones

Farmingdale, NJ
July 25, 1864
My Dear Brother,

Thomas, as this is a stormy morning, you would think by looking at pasture fields that it was October weather instead of July. All of our Christian neighbors have been praying for rain and at last it has come. It rained very hard all night and this morning [it] is still raining. Father says it will do a great deal of good to the corn and potatoes and to the pasture. Last Friday a fire broke out in

Hankinson's swamp between Joseph Degill's [?] and Farmingdale. It is still burning, or was, if this rain has not put it out. It has burned hundreds of acres already, the weather being very dry. The fire broke out in six different directions all at the same time. At John Aldrige's pipe there were fifty wartberry pickers in the swamp. Some of our fair neighbors were down there and I imagine they all ran. Sam Degill's wife came near to being burned since she is hard of hearing in one ear and deaf in the other. They had to pull her through the fire to get her out. It came through the fields to Joseph Corlie's farm but did no damage. Mrs. Brown has had a letter from Peter. He is a prisoner in Richmond.[55] He has had his left arm amputated. I can not tell you any particulars of the letter. He was wounded several days before he was picked up. His letter was written by someone else. I am safe yet. I am a lucky fellow, don't you think so? I feel sorry for Peter though, poor fellow. He will fret himself to death. This letter is the last one received from William. Maggie received a letter from you Saturday night. We were all glad you are well and glad to think your time is so nearly up. I do wish William's time was up too, but it is not so. I am everyday more sorry about John, but there is no use in regretting it now. John C. Patterson was not as badly wounded as reported. The bullet struck his pocket book. He sent it home since it saved his life. The ball then struck his book and glanced across his stomach. There is no news now of any importance. You wished to know how the crops are and I have told you how dry it was. You can imagine how everything is scorched up. Jimmie has a lame arm – he is awfully afraid of the draft.

_____ Jones

---

[55]Libby Prison in Richmond was one of the most famous POW compounds in the Civil War. By this time most of the prisoners, Union soldiers, had been shifted southward to Andersonville, Georgia, site of the infamous Camp Sumter. Eventually this site would house over 40,000 Union soldiers, 13,000 of whom would die.

Before Petersburg
July 29, 1864
Dear Parents,

As this is a fine and glorious morning I thought I would pen you a few lines to let you know how I am getting along. A siege of this city is progressing every day and we are in one respect out-digging them. We are in close quarters all the time but as usual, I lay low. We have not had any more casualties in our camp since I last told you and I hope we will endeavor to keep it so. You must let me know who has been drafted in your next letter so I can have a fine laugh. John C. Patterson was badly wounded. My time would have been up but for re-enlisting. But what is to be will be. I might have been killed at the battle at Cemetary Hill but all for the best.

Your affectionate brother,
William Jones

Hammond General Hospital
Ward No. 15
Point Lookout, Maryland
August 10, 1864
Friend Thomas;

The whole division has been released from their position in front of Petersburg and now are back at Bermuda Hundred. They fought nearly all day on the 30th and that night they crossed the Appomattox River and marched to Bermuda Hundred on the following day. The sun was awful, and because of the heat, several dropped dead on the roadside. In the fighting on the 30th Major Swartwout was killed. He had just received a commission as major. The First Sergeant McDougall was killed in Co. C and several others that I can't think of at the present. William came out safely once more. He is a lucky boy is all I can say for him & I hope he may be as fortunate in the time to come as he has been in the past. Oh, dear Thomas, if you were here sometimes to hear the political arguments. They nearly come to blows with their canes and crutches. I say let's have it ended somehow, if they do ever intend to close this bloody scene, for it would be too bad to have the curses of another long year to fight. Now you see the Rebels are in Maryland and Pennsylvania again.[56] I can't see what they are thinking in this present time of crisis.

Now Thomas, I can't think of much more worth saying except that there was a great wind, like a tornado, which came down the river about six o'clock in the morning. It struck the Commissary Department and tore the whole house down. It then went down to the beach and tore down another building. It then lifted a sutler's shanty right off the ground and carried it for about 20 feet. It destroyed some more little wharves and now there are about 500 pieces of timber all around. It crossed the Point, entered the Bay and then worked its way over to the Hundred and crossed the shores of Virginia. It was the hardest wind I ever saw in my life and it even wounded some men. It hurt one man who was on guard at the time. He was lifted into the air fell with such force that he broke his leg in three places. I believe that he has since died.

From your ever true friend,
John D. Cottrell

USS North Carolina
August 11, 1864
Friend Maggie,

An old friend wished me to go in the navy with him. I received $200 cash down as a bounty and will get $33 more in government bounty every three months. This pen is so poor it won't hold ink. You will please answer this letter to let me know all the news.

From Your Old Friend,
John D. Fogerty
Brooklyn, NY

---

[56] This is another reference to Confederate General Jubal Early's raid on Washington.

Pensacola, Florida
Letter Not Dated – Probably August 1864
Dear Maggie,

This will make the third letter I have written and I have received no answer. I have no doubt you are somewhat surprised at my decision to join the Navy again. Well now, I will explain things to you. When I got in the boat going to New York, I met with an old friend and we decided to join up together. This will make the third time for both of us. We got down in time to help capture Mobile. Only thirty were killed. We will have to go help take Galveston, too.

I should much rather be home' going home with you from church on a Sunday [as it] would look much nicer. I have just been working very hard getting the captain's boat ready to put in the water; it's a cutter. The flag ship, the *Hartford* left here yesterday for home. The cheering went on for a little while.[57]

Dear Maggie, I'll come home again. I think I will come to a close. Give my love to all the family and a little bit for yourself, if not more, don't you think so? Please answer this right away!!

John P. Fogerty
U.S. Ship *Potomac*, Pensacola, Florida

Farmingdale, NJ
August 12, 1864
My Dear Brother Thomas

I wish, Thomas, that William was coming home with you but that will not be. It was the worst thing he ever did when he enlisted for another term. Have you heard anything from that Navy arrange-

---

[57] Fogerty's ship, the *Potomac* was among the original escort ships which took the 48th to Port Royal. The *Hartford* is interesting because this was Admiral David Farragut's vessel and it was at the Battle of Mobile Bay in August of 1864 that he issued the famous command, "Damn the torpedoes! Full speed ahead!"

ment? I hope you will see if Strickland has had an answer before you come home. I am sorry now that I asked him to write – I am afraid he will not put himself to any great exertion to use his influence. I am in hopes he will. I hope you will know if anything has been done before you come home. It will be a satisfaction to know the worst.

I for my part feel very anxious about him as his letters are of the most despondent and gloomy kind. I hope he will not be tempted to do anything imprudent. You must write a very cheerful letter to him before you come home. We have sent him tobacco and stamps this week and are going to send him some money., as his last letter stated he was out of both money and tobacco. Brother thinks he will be paid off while he is in Bermuda Hundred. I hope he will. We have heard nothing from him since Saturday night. Maggie received a letter from you on Saturday night. That was an awful fight he was in the last of July.[58] I for my part can not see how he came through so safely. I hope the Almighty who is the soldier's friend will keep him from danger. Thomas, it is time the 10th Corps had a change, do you not think so? I think they have had a long time of hard living and no rest. I hope they will have a rest from what keeps William in such sour spirits. Haddie wants to know if you will be home this year for peaches. I tell her I hope so. Corn looks pretty good considering the dry weather we have had. Try and write the day before you come home if you can and tell us where to meet you.

To Thomas from your ever loving sister to death,
Good bye, Janie

Chesterfield County, Virginia
Letter not dated but probably late summer, 1864
Friend Maggie,

I am glad to hear that you are well at present. I am afraid that the draft will seriously affect some of the West Farms gentlemen.

---

[58] This reference is to the Battle of the Crater, fought in the trenches of Petersburg on July 30, 1864.

I heard that W.H. Smith had been captured – and he said that he would never be taken prisoner! He has been caught and at least I hope he will be satisfied with his jailer. We have been on picket since yesterday morning. We just got into camp about sundown. We are to move our camp a mile or so nearer to the front at three o'clock tomorrow morning and have general inspection at eight o'clock. Our company has lost ten or twelve men killed, wounded, and missing since we came here. The West Farms boys are all right. I believe I received a letter from Thomas. He is well except for his arm. There has been no general engagement since last Monday. The enemy has made several desperate charges on our breastworks and they were repulsed with considerable loss. The pickets were firing at one another occasionally during the day. The weather is quite warm here. At present the roads have been in very bad order on account of the recent rain. There have been some very fine fields of wheat and corn growing here but they are trampled down. We are encamped in a wheat field about eight miles from Bermuda Hundred. We heard the enemy was throwing up earth works in sight of ours. The pickets of both sides are close enough to speak one another and they see each other all day long. Calvin Havens was over here in the tent a few nights ago. He looks well and he is in the 18th Corps as a teamster. Some very laughable incidents sometimes occur amid a fight or skirmish. I understand the enemy sent in a flag of truce to give us seven hours to leave here, but General Butler informed them that he gave them seven minutes to leave our lines and the conference ended there. They throw shell and solid [shot] over once in a while but do no damage. We have a strong position. One battery of light artillery went home today. They were discharged; their time was up yesterday.

We have heard that General Sherman has whipped General Johnston and captured 32 pieces of cannon and was on the march to Atlanta. There are rumors that the Rebels have been at work in South Carolina. Have you heard what damage they have done? All is quiet at the front. I hope we can rest all night for once. We have also heard that General Grant has whipped General Lee again and had turned his flank. I hope the war will be over before long. I think there will be some happy boys at that time. We have plenty of duty to do around here and we are all hearty and strong yet, for I think it is healthier here than it was down in South Carolina.

You must excuse this dirty paper as it is about the last I have and it has been in my knapsack for some time. You know soldiers cannot keep things quite as tidy as they would at home. I must close as the drums are beating tatoo. Give my respects to [all]. I remain as ever your true friend till death.

John A. Woodside
Company D. 48-Reg.
2 Brigade 2 Division 10 Army Corps, Virginia

Letter Not Dated
Quarters, Army of the Potomac before Petersburg, Virginia
Friend Maggie,

After a lapse of time I try to answer your kind and ever welcome letter. We are all in as good health as circumstances will permit. We are under fire most of the time. I think we are in more danger here from shot and shell than we would be at the front for the shells all pass over us there and strike in the rear where we are now lying. One came over just a few moments ago and killed and wounded five men that belong to the 26th. There have been none of us hit or hurt by their shell or shot yet, but we don't know when we will get a crack from some of them. We have been fortunate so far. I hope I will be as fortunate for the next 60 days and then I think can get out of range by going far enough to the rear. Sergeant John H. Graham was killed by a sharp shooter on the 30th of June and George W. Richman was killed by a sharpshooter on the 1st of July. We have had one man wounded. That is our total loss since we have been here. We are living in holes dug in the hillside so the shot has its strength at the top of the hill and they rebound and drop nearly straight down afterwards before they can hit us. There have been several which have passed over since I commenced this letter. They strike the houses in front of us and one passed through a tree of good size. There was one man who had the whole side of his head take off by a shell and another who had his arm badly shattered by the same shell when it burst. It happened last night when we were in the mortar battery. Before we were relieved the Rebs commenced shelling and dropped a shell in a trench in our rear and killed the two men I have just spoken about. They belonged to the 3rd New York. They dropped two more in the battery in front of us. One hit a bunker, but it did not burst. The other struck on top of a trench and burst, sprinkling us with dirt but hurt no one. We can see the church spires of Petersburg quite plainly from our works. We have my Blakely and three or four 32-pound Parrot guns[59] mounted on a hill and they are called the Petersburg Express. They throw shot and shell every five or ten minutes into the city. We have been doing it since we arrived here. The Rebs had a ball over there one night this week. We could hear the band playing till our Express opened and that soon quieted them. We set the city afire one night and we could hear the fire bells ringing quite plainly. There was quite a _____ throughout the city. Our pickets and the Rebs pickets are about 40 yards apart and that is plenty close enough. Every day the weather is quite hot and uncomfortable. Being very dry and dusty, one can not move without passing a cloud of dust. There has been some rumors of our being relieved from here. I hope it is so, for we need a good rest. We have been in the field since the first of February and have seen a considerable part of the country.

The Rebs made a charge yesterday evening on the right and were repulsed with losses. There was a charge made on the left but I have heard nothing reliable from that quarter. That was rather a doleful letter you last wrote. I don't know what makes the folks at home so downhearted and discouraged while the troops in the field are as

---

59 Blakely and Parrott guns were both rifled cannon, hence capable of greater range and accuracy than traditional smoothbores. Blakely guns were made in England and used by the Confederate forces more than they were by Union batteries. They were considered "heavy guns" and were often used in siege warfare or coastal defenses. Parrott guns were similar, but were used more extensively in the war. They had a tendency to burst, however, and manufacture of the Parrotts ceased after 1865. Many of these guns could range three miles or more.

cheerful and contented as if they were enjoying the best of times. The Rebs throw quite a number of shot and shell at us but they don't do much damage. Our mortar shells tear them all upside down and hurt quite a number of the Rebs. One was blown 20 feet in the air by one of our shells the other night. Our boys drop them inside their works with every shot they make. I had a letter from John D. He is doing very well. From what he says, Connover Emmons is doing well in Baltimore. I am now anxiously watching and looking for the cooks for supper. The Sanitary Commission gives us picked cabbage, canned tomatoes, pickles, and dried apples. We get fresh bread twice a week but it is pretty hard when we get it. We hear it rumored that part of Lee's army has gone toward Pennsylvania and have taken possession of Harper's Ferry, Virginia. I think we have troops enough around Washington to defend it and keep out the Rebs without much trouble. General [Quincy R.] Gillmore has been confirmed as a major general and has command of the defenses around Washington. There is only our division left of our Corps here. Well, I have finished my supper of bitter coffee and dried apple. I saved and washed the dishes, or cups rather, as dishes are scarce articles about here. The effects of artillery show plainly everywhere we go. You will see trees marked by shot and houses all smashed up and [in] desolation. Everywhere one goes there were fine fields of wheat and oats, but they are all destroyed by our troops marching over and camping in them. I think we have got John in a tight place now. It is a question of time about getting the city of Petersburg for Grant has used the same plan that he did at Vicksburg. He didn't care too much about the city. He wants to get the army and put an end to it at once. I will now close as we are likely to move at any moment.

Friends yourself included, I remain as ever your friend.
John A. Woodside
Write Soon!

Hammond General Hospital
Ward No. 15
Point Lookout
August 23, 1864
Friend Maggie,

I heard from the regiment this morning. They have been in some hard fights. My company lost ten men and a lieutenant. Lieutenant Tantum was killed and his body fell into the hands of the Rebels. But William is alright. I believe that all of the boys from our place are alright. I had a letter from John A. Woodside. I saw they were near Ft. Darling. I asked how our brigade was making out and whether they had been in any fight yet or not. I am looking for a letter every day. I hope I shall get one this morning from the regiment. The regiment has only got three officers left. The rest are all killed or wounded. Maggie, why has your pen been still so long? Don't fail me; I shall soon close as my slate is full; also I don't know what to write about because of my not hearing from you in so long.

Your ever true friend and faithful 'til last,
John D. Cottrell
Goodbye. Please answer soon.

Before Petersburg, Virginia
August 31, 1864
Dear Sister,

Last Sabbath we left Bermuda Hundred to come to Petersburg, again. We occupy the same portion of the line that the 18th Corps has. Our brigade lies just a little to the right of where we were before only we do not have as many men as we had before. We hold the Weldon Railroad after much hard fighting. We [just] lay still and force Johnny Reb to come out and fight. We have had enough men slaughtered trying to bring them out of their strongholds so they must try and dislodge our army from the Weldon Railroad or they can't winter their armies in Virginia. At present the picket firing is going on as brisk as ever and the mortar batteries have their sport throwing shells into Petersburg. I sat up on a hill the night before last and it was a pretty sight to see the shells going through the air and exploding in the city.[60] We have had no casualties in our regiment. John Woodside is getting better. I suppose it is because his time is nearly up. I would like you to ask him when he comes home how many battles he has been in. Let me know what he says. The only battles he has been in is the battle of Olustee and the skirmish we had up in Pocotaligo in South Carolina. In Virginia he has been in none at all but he can eat more than any man in Co. D. We have been in more battles since we came to Virginia than you could shake a stick at. I think I am luckier than all of them to come through without a scratch. I am in hopes of getting home this winter.

William Jones

South Ballston, NY
September 5 1864
My Dearest Maggie:

I am at home, brother Aaron is in heaven, and brother Henry is one of the noble ones who are assisting in putting down this wicked rebellion. Brother Johnnie is in Michigan in business for himself, brother Roscius is in Camden, a clerk in a grocery store. The two younger ones are at home. Yes, Maggie this deep affliction, due to the loss of a son and a brother loving and faithful, has come upon us. God, our loving Father, helps us. An earthly tie is broken, but

---

[60] General U.S. Grant became very skilled at siege warfare during the Civil War, evidence his successful captures of Vicksburg and Petersburg. One of his tactics was to bring in heavy coastal siege mortars and artillery to reduce enemy bastions and morale. One of the most famous guns at Petersburg was the heavy mortar, "The Dictator," a photograph of its replica, still in place at Petersburg National Military Park, is shown in the photo section of this book.

broken here only to add anther attraction in Heaven. Yes, we have the assurances that our loved one was taken from us because our Father loved us and him. And he is safe with Him now waiting for us. And shall we surely go when our work, like his, is finished here. This is the first time death has come to us. It is a dear price to pay for our country. But Maggie, it was given in love. Thank God! Our brother was a patriot. Oh, what more honored name than Patriot and Christian. His work was done. Therefore we grieve not that he had his reward a few days before us.

His body lies under the shadow of a large butternut tree, not far from Spotsylvania Courthouse. He was buried respectfully by a few of his comrades and the chaplin. Maggie, we do not feel like murmuring. How many have been much more afflicted? The tidings which your letter bore of Mr. Peter Brown's family was all news to me. I hadn't heard a word about them since I left Jersey. Not many families have escaped the dreadful effects of this war. We received a letter from brother Henry tonight. He is not far from Harper's Ferry. He wrote that he was well, and that was the 2nd of July.

Ever your true Friend,
Mary

Hammond General Hospital
Ward No. 10
Point Lookout, Maryland
September 11, 1864
Friend Thomas,

You say the 5th was the last day to give the young man a chance to enlist and now he will have to stand the draft. I hope old Honest Abraham will _____ the draft _____ and fetch them out first. They want all the men that can be gotten. Let Grant walk into Richmond for now Sherman is in Atlanta and if Grant can only manage to either take the city or else destroy the Danville [Rail]road. Then the Confederacy is cut in two and it will slowly give up if Lee's army is destroyed. The Southern Confederacy would be gone and they could just count themselves a set of condemned rebels. I heard from the regiment this morning that they are in front of Petersburg and are having good times, too. They say that there was much firing on the lines in the front of the 10th Corps but the 2nd Corps is near the Weldon Railroad and the Rebs are concentrating all their forces in that direction with the intention of keeping our forces from getting to the Danville Road. Fool Lee's Headquarters is near the Weldon Railroad and he will make some hard fighting before he lets Grant take that other road. If he does get it, all of the communications [will be] destroyed between Lee and the rest of the Southern states. Then his supplies will all be gone. There is not much more I can tell you. Of the soldiers here, if a man would speak of Honest Abraham, he must speak very low or else someone will hear him and that man will get his head hurt for it.

From your ever true friend,
John D. Cottrell

By Petersburg, Virginia
September 12, 1864
Dear Sister,

Yours of the South. The old man will start for home probably tomorrow. When John Woodside comes home, tell Mother she must cook him a very fine dinner or supper or whatever it may be, and tell him to bring it to me. John will have a very good chance to judge whether he is a sick man or a man that is recovering from a severe shock of the shell fever. But just bring that vacant bed in for I think it will be vacant for years to come. You must please excuse me for giving you recommendations as he is going to be your guest for a day or two, till he goes home.

I am very sad to hear that Miss Brather had such a misfortune in the war.

I hope it will never be my fate to serve on the pistol line for most who fall on the pistol line are dead men.

George W. Richman was shot when he was on the top of the bank to fire a shot. He was shot through the head at distance of about 200 yards. A man who has a stiff back won't live long here.

You say you are waiting for the draft, well, I am not, for I am waiting for the war to end. Some are not coming without the draft. I wish they would all die at home. Let them all die contented and go to hell in a batch together.

You will probably not like this letter, but it is the best I can do for you at the present.

I have shouted enough for this time.

As mother used to say, a wink is as good as a nod to a blind horse.

Yours truly,
William Jones

Fort Schuyler, New York
September, 17 1864
Dear Maggie,

I arrived here this morning. I got my pass yesterday without any trouble. I went to Brooklyn looking for a boarding house. Thomas met me at the hospital door today. His arm is healing fast and very nicely.

I was surprised to see it look so well. He is going to try for a pass soon. It will only be for 24 hours. He has written to William with his left hand.

His stimulant now is whiskey. I brought him some wine and he says it was the best he ever tasted. Maggie, if you or father think of coming next week, write early in the week if you please and let Thomas know when or if you intend to come. It is more than likely that he will go home with you. If you don't intend on coming let Thomas and me know. The men are up and going to have their beds made. They are going to have their wounds dressed so I am secluded in a little room.

From Janie

Hammond General Hospital
Point Lookout, Maryland
October, 1864
Friend Thomas,

I am glad to hear your arm [is] soothing you so well for I was afraid it would prove to be a failure. I hope I may get to see you for they have put me in the invalid care and I shan't see many Rebel bullets for the rest of my time that I have to serve. I don't think that my time will last over one year if our army is victorious. The Rebels are now in a great stew and if Georgia will come back into the Union,[61] the Southern Confederacy is cut two and certainly they can't hold out much longer.

Sheridan is foiling Early's Rebel force[62] and if he is successful and captures the rest of the force the Rebels will be pretty well

---

[61] By late 1863 and early 1864 Georgia officials, most notably Governor Joseph E. Brown and Senator Robert Toombs, had become highly dissatisfied with the administration of Jefferson Davis. In effect, they began to form an opposition party in the Confederate congress. Their criticisms not only stemmed from a personal dislike to Mr. Davis, but also from such government policies as the draft and the suspension of the writ of habeas corpus. It was rumored that Georgia toyed with secession from the CSA.

[62] This reference is to Sheridan's famous ride at the 3rd Battle of Winchester. As his forces began reeling back after an attack by Jubal Early, "Little Phil" mounted his famous horse Rienzi and rode through the lines at breakneck speed. The mere image of their commander galloping to the front rallied his men. Sheridan, victorious, then proceeded to devastate the entire Shenandoah Valley by burning barns and farms and destroying livestock to the extent that if a crow should fly through the Valley, "it would need provisions." This was the last major action in the Shenandoah Valley.

played out. More than that, everything is coming to our standard as fast as it can. Yes everything is coming down – the politicians of both north and south are coming down, gold and silver are coming down. The gold in the southern states has gone down so far that the bankers of the so-called Confederacy will not pay gold at any price for Rebel money. The peace party is coming down, so is Fernando Wood and the rest of his friends like Horace Greeley and Gov. Brown and I believe all that is needed now to end this cruel war is for Grant to make one grand success, destroy the Lynchburg [Rail]road, and the so-called Confederacy is down.

You speak of a young gentleman getting married. I believe I know the gentleman very well. I wish him luck. Thomas, how does the election go in Monmouth County? I think the whole of the Southern Confederacy is coming down and I hope I am right, for it is time. You say there is not going to be a draft. There will soon be a move made on Wilmington [North Carolina] I think and there can't be a large Rebel force there to oppose them unless Hood or a part of his force is there and I don't think he can spare many of them.

I see in the papers from Rebel forces that Beauregard is going to release Hood from his command and he will try to stop Sherman. There are a great many refugees a-coming [through] our lines, men, women, and children. They say they are starving in Richmond.[63]

John D. Cottrell
Goodbye!

---

[63] Two items in this letter deserve clarification. One relates to the inflation rates to which the Confederate dollar were subject. Some sources suggest an inflation rate of 9,000 percent; this compares to a Northern inflation rate of sixty-four percent. Secondly, John Bell Hood's army, rather than confront Sherman's force on its "March to the Sea," attempted to draw him out of Georgia by attacking Union strongholds in Tennessee. Hood's army was recklessly destroyed at Franklin and Nashville in November and December of 1864.

Jones Landing, Virginia
October 30, 1864
Dear Brother,

I have told you about my being away from the company and regiment now. I hope to stay away. I am driving a team and up at the front every other day. I like my new position first rate and I hope to have six mules to drive soon. I could have had a position in the company but a position doesn't save you from the fighting. This job that I now have keeps me well to the rear pretty much all the time. The sick and wounded now in the hospitals are all going home on furlough. I think that there is a going to be a forward movement before the election. They have been fighting all week. The result is rumored around here that the Danville [rail]Road was taken & [there were] four thousand prisoners. If it is true, the Rebs will soon be played out and we can be home soon. I don't care, for I am tired of it all.[64]

I get letters frequently from G.W. Thompson. He is home in his father's store. He sent me his card and an officer in the 48th wrote him and asked him if he could write to him as well as me. But G.W.T. told him that I was the only one in the regiment he had cared for before he was discharged. He was tired of soldiering. He almost cried out when I told him I reenlisted. If I had taken his advice I would not be here now, but all for the best. He and I are going out to California when our time is up.

Affectionately,
Brother William

---

[64] Grant ordered assaults east of Richmond and southwest of Petersburg on October 27-28. Although the strategic results were marginal, the tactical result was another tightening of the noose around Lee's army and the further attrition of his forces. This movement can be seen as an envelopment that weakened Lee's center by further stretching his thinning line.

Dutchfields
October, 1864
Dear Parents and more,

I sit myself down for a few lines. I'd like to inform you that I am well. There are sixteen of us here and we can have a little money to buy stuff that we can use. I will keep forty dollars and I paid out twelve and lent nineteen to twenty dollars of it. As for the nineteen to twenty dollars I lent, you will see that it will comes back the next pay day. I could not well refuse the boys that I lent the money to.

I had never spoken a word to anybody about driving a team of horses. But one day this brigade wagon master came to me and asked if I would like to drive a team. First rate, Bill says. He and I sent our names into the Brigade Head Quarters and I was detailed to this. It will leave me some distance to the rear and a good ways out of danger. I liked it at first that I drive four horses and will have four mules soon. One thing is that I am out of money now and my jelly is infested with bugs and maggots.

I have a good job now and one that I like having. I mean to keep out of the company as long as I can.

author unknown

Point Lookout, Maryland
November 3, 1864
Dear Maggie,

Maggie, you say you are busily engaged in teaching? If so, please tell me where. You say that in the school day there is no time? Only for study? I will agree with you there and as you have said, Sunday is the only day you can call your own. Now Maggie, I see it's always the news of William. He is well. I heard from him the other day. He has got a good job with the Quartermaster and this will keep him clear of going to the front and to battle. And I hope that he may stay there, for he has had plenty of the front for one man. Few men have seen as much of the field as he. You say it is bad to think that they put me in the invalid corps. I am very well contented at the present and I don't believe I shall ever be sent to any invalid regiment. I think I shall stay here and get a good job here at headquarters. If I take good care of myself this winter, I shall be alright in the spring. You say Calvin Havens and John A. Woodside have both paid you a visit.

You say there are very busy times here? There is great excitement all about the election. I hope Little Mac carries the day and if my vote will help him any, I shall help him some. You ask me if I am about to get a furlough. I am always ready to take a furlough if it would be granted me. And I shall try and get a furlough this winter if I can. Please excuse this short letter of mine and I will try to do better in the next one.

> From your friend,
> John D. Cottrell
> Please write soon.

Jones Landing, Virginia
November 16, 1864
Dear Sister,

I received a letter from John D. [Cottrell] the day before yesterday. He is well and says that he has good quarters and has everything comfortable. I am very glad that he is the _____ _____. That is just the place to keep out of the way of bullets. I will be kept out of the way of them, too and that will suit me for I am done fighting.

I hope Mac is elected, but I don't hardly believe he will.[65] Nothing to do but take care of my horses.

> Remaining Your Brother William

---

[65] The election returns of 1864 showed that fully 80 percent of soldiers in the Union armies voted for Lincoln. Interestingly, the Democratic peace candidate, former General George McClellan, did succeed in carrying New Jersey.

Point Lookout, Maryland
November 7, 1864
Friend Maggie,

If I should happen to get home, I should call and pay you a visit.
Well, I think I hear you say, "Friend John, tomorrow will be the end
of the war and the political strife; the long and ancient day that has
been so longly awaited, with an eye of interest and anxiety—the
great day of election." Tomorrow is the day and then you, as well as
me and all, will know who either makes, or rather restores, the
union and makes peace. For I don't think that Old Abraham is the
man to do this.

The men who would vote the McClellan ticket were kept here and
only Old A.'s men was sent to their states to vote. All of the
McClellan men were kept here. I suppose I might have gotten home
if I would have said I should vote for A.

But never. I would sooner stay here for another year than to
come home and vote for him, but I guess I shall be alright, for a
furlough about Christmas or New Year's would suit me better and I
should enjoy it a great deal. For William, I will try to get him to get a
furlough about the same time. Now my friend Maggie, I shall close
this, and if I get a chance to write anymore before I send it, I will.
And if not, please excuse all of the mistakes.

From your ever true friend,
John D. Cottrell

Letter not dated, probably late November 1864
Part 2nd

Now Maggie, you speak of getting a furlough and coming home
this winter. I hope I shall and if I can, I will jump at the chance. I
hope that William can get a furlough at the same time. For, oh,
would it not be beautiful to be home together. I think I hear you as
well as my folks say, I wish they could. And now if General Sherman
is only successful and gets to his destination. The Rebels will all be

bothered pretty well and I think that his advance will take the Rebel capital and destroy the Southern Confederacy. If this plan should meet with success it will be the greatest stroke to the Rebels, just provided [that] the army gets through to the sea.[66] I see in this morning's paper that he has gotten between Augusta and Savannah and liberated a lot of our prisoners that have been suffering for many months at the hands of the Rebels. He has armed all that was fit to be armed. Grant is expected to make a move any day. I don't believe that the Army of the Potomac is intending to move until they find out how Sherman is making out. Now that Father Abraham has the chair for another four years it is all for the best.

Your Ever True Friend,
John D. Cottrell

Point Lookout, Maryland
November 27, 1864
Friend Margaret,

This pleasant Sabbath morning I once more, after over a week's silence, embrace the few leisure moments that I have to pen you a few words, though they may not be at all interesting to you for the very good reason that the news is all dull here. Only the news of General Sherman and that appears to be very good. If he is successful it will be a great fall to the Rebels.

Well, Margaret, Thanksgiving is passed and I must say that it was enjoyed here by all. There were all kinds of amusement and a splendid dinner was arranged. At night there were two good musical bands that passed around and played splendidly. I only hope that if I

---

[66] This is a reference to William Tecumseh Sherman's famous March to the Sea that took place in November and December of 1864. He arrived in the outskirts of Savannah just before Christmas, completing one of the most remarkable campaigns in military history cutting a sixty-mile wide swath of destruction through the state of Georgia.

have to spend Christmas and New Year's here, they may pass off as good as this Thanksgiving day has.[67]

John D. Cottrell
To his friend, Miss M.E.J.

Point Lookout, Maryland
December 2, 1864
My Friend Maggie,

I hope you will please excuse me for reprimanding you for not writing. I will give you my word as a friend that I will never be guilty of such a thing again. I beg you to forgive me for what I said. I will never forgive myself for doing such a thing. The last letter I got from you said that you were teaching school and I am overjoyed to hear of such luck to my friend and I hope you may succeed.

Unsigned, but probably John D. Cottrell

Point Lookout, Maryland
December 18, 1864
My Friend Margaret E.J.,

Allow me this fine morning to favor you with a few lines. I suppose you will hear of the particulars of the fall of Savannah before this letter will reach you. General Sherman has taken [the city], its forts, and everything around there. He has 13,000 prisoners and over 200 pieces of artillery. He took Ft. McAllister which [was built] on the Ogeechee River 15 miles from Savannah. After a fight of _____ hours[68] the Rebels surrendered. A part of his force crossed the Savannah River and, with a part of Kilpatrick's cavalry, is marching toward Charleston. They have already cooperated with General

---

[67] Thanksgiving was formally made a national holiday by President Lincoln only the year before, in 1863.

[68] The fight to capture Ft. McAllister actually lasted less than one-half hour late in the afternoon of December 13, 1864.

Foster's forces at _____ and they will follow the railroad to Charleston.

I think [that] the next news will be that General Thomas has captured the whole of General Hood's army and the whole country will be clear of Rebels.

There is good news from every place [in] the Department of Tennessee. The Rebel General Hood attacked General Thomas and drove him back for some distance [before] the lines of battle were reformed.[69] The fight raged very heavy for some time and then the Rebels fell back. Thomas captured 15 pieces of artillery and 5000 prisoners.

Another force of ours started from _____, encountered the Rebel General Price and routed his force, capturing half of his wagon train.

From Your Affectionate Friend,
John D. Cottrell

Chester Point, Virginia
Letter not dated, but probably late 1864
Dear Sister,

As I lean on my knapsack this pleasant morning, I write you a few lines to let you know all the particulars.

Last Tuesday we got paid. I received 50 dollars of government bounty and I got all that was due to me but $10. I will send home $60 on Monday or Tuesday.[70]

---

[69] Cottrell is mistaken. Schofield's lines at Franklin faced a frontal assault from Hood, inflicted nearly fifty percent casualties and then executed a strategic retrograde movement back to Nashville. Hood followed and again attacked but to no avail. He then had to face the full brunt of George Thomas's nearly intact army of over 50,000. Hood's valiant, yet decimated force was under 30,000, probably closer to 23,000. There was little doubt as to the outcome when Thomas counter-attacked on December 15.

[70] A private in the Union Army in the Civil War was paid $13-16 per month.

We are up the York River right near Yorktown. So we are not in the Army of the Potomac.

Yours ever,
William Jones

Point Lookout
December 25, 1864
Kind Friend Maggie,

Allow me to wish you a Merry Christmas, for it has passed as a smooth leg on a beautiful day. It is now 3 pm and the church bell has just rung.

I promised to tell you what our grand Christmas dinner was composed of. I can tell you it was a very good one and was ornamented with splendid groans of all kinds. As for the dinner it was good, plenty of everything to eat and drink. First there were roast turkeys, chicken and beef, and all kinds of vegetables you would want; plenty of pies, cakes and puddings, bread and butter, and as for the drink there was both coffee and tea, cider and ale beer and last of all, I must say, some egg nog. You could get all you wished of anything, and the day so far has passed very well. This is a bill of fare for the Grand Christmas dinner prepared for the soldiers at Point Lookout, Md.

Now Margaret, this is a gay way for a soldier boy to pass away the hours of a Christmas afternoon while many of the young chaps have gone to Church. Yet I can content myself here in penning you a few lines instead of going to church.

The rumor from the regiment's paper is that the Rebels are going to send missioners [sic] for peace.[71] The Rebels are getting awfully

---

[71] On February 3, 1865 CSA Vice-President Alexander H. Stevens met with President Lincoln aboard the *River Queen* in what was informally known as the Hampton Roads (VA) Conference. Talks failed as the Union position was inflexible on matters concerning slavery and the restoration of the United States. Again, however, it is surprising how accurate the rumor mill was during the Civil War.

down because their president Mr. Davis blames all the defeats of the army on mismanagement. There are complaints of awful suffering in all parts of the South. Maggie, I heard from the regiment the other day. They have gone and I have heard they have already arrived at Beaufort, South Carolina. I suppose that Wilmington is the next place they will strike. William is well. My sheet is full and I shall close leaving you with my best wishes for your welfare and happiness.

From your affectionate friend,
John Cottrell

Point Lookout, Maryland
January 3, 1865
Friend Maggie,

I haven't heard from the regiment in some time, but I had a letter from a fellow who belongs to the regiment. The news he gives is that the regiment had gone down to North Carolina and they left all of their drummers and fifers behind them in their old camp at Deep Bottom, Virginia. He had not heard from them yet and that was on the 27th of December. Now, Maggie, please tell me how you passed your time on New Year's. If you hear from William tell me how he is and all of the news. Now you must please excuse a short letter for I haven't got anything to tell you this time. My health is very good now and I think by Spring I shall be able to go on duty again. If I do I shall try to get to my old regiment, if I can.

From your affectionate friend
J.D. Cottrell

Chapter Five

1865

Fort Fisher to Petersburg

On December 8, 1864, the 48th left its trenches at Petersburg to take part in the Union army's attempt to take Fort Fisher, at the mouth of the Cape Fear River in North Carolina. General Ben Butler's assault during the last week of December ended in dismal failure and Butler's dismissal. The 48th returned to Bermuda Hundred and, after a brief respite, to Ft. Fisher where it participated in the fort's capture in mid-January. As the regimental history notes, it is both significant and ironic that the 48th took part in assaults on two of the Confederacy's most heavily defended coastal strongholds, Fts. Wagner and Fisher.

The Battle of Fort Fisher

Straddling a peninsula jutting into the northern flank of the wide bay comprising the mouth of the Cape Fear River in North Carolina stood Fort Fisher. Located eighteen miles south of the city of Wilmington, the fort silently and ominously guarded the river and the city to maintain the final port of entry for Confederate blockade runners. In many ways, the fort represented the dying Confederacy's last hope in the winter of 1864-65.

As Grant's forces continued to press Lee at Petersburg and Sherman was poised for his invasion of the Carolinas, the port of Wilmington had literally become a lifeline. Besides the fact that the blockade runners continued to slip past the 500-ship Federal navy (the odds of capture have been estimate at one-in-three by late 1864), the city also connected Weldon, NC and ultimately Petersburg, VA by rail. Confederate government reports estimated that, in the last nine weeks of 1864, 8.6 million pounds of meat, 1.5 million pounds of lead, two million pounds of saltpeter, 546,000 pairs of shoes, 69,000 rifles and forty-three cannon and more were supplied to Rebel forces through Charleston and Wilmington alone.[72] Charleston was tightly blockaded, so most of these supplies came through Wilmington. The capture of Fort Fisher and Wilmington, would seal off the Confederacy and represent the final chapter for the entire coastal campaign.

The indefatigable Gen. Benjamin Butler was given the first shot at Fort Fisher. On December 20, 1864 the federal navy was spotted. Butler had arrived with not only a 6500-man landing force, but also the *Louisiana*, a hulk filled with 200 tons of powder. Butler's imaginative plan was to detonate the ship within 300 yards of the fort's sand-dune palisade. Then, if a landing force was even necessary, he would invest the fort from the landward side, north of the fort's embrasures. In the early morning hours of Christmas Eve Day, the *Louisiana* exploded after a curious, maddening delay. However, the pilot had erroneously dropped anchor 600 yards from the shoreline and the ship drifted harmlessly before exploding well north of the fort. Nevertheless, Butler landed some 2,500 men on Christmas Day, but lacking confidence, he hastily withdrew.

Thus, the first attempt to take the fort was a dismal failure and Butler went the way of his "powder boat" plan. Butler was relieved and returned to politics. He would later figure prominently in the Reconstruction Congress as a Radical Republican.

Realizing the necessity of capturing the fort, General Alfred H. Terry made it his business to complete the unfinished work. With some sixty naval vessels and a 9,000-man landing force, he invested the fort on January 13, 1865. His naval guns opened fire at 7:19 A.M. and pounded the fort for the duration of the daylight hours while

---

[72] Shelby Foote, *The Civil War: A Narrative History* (New York: Random House, 1974) 3:741.

Terry's landing party slogged ashore north of the fort. The Confederate commander William Lamb, had no more than 2,000 troops to oppose him.

The Union plan for the ground assault called for a dual attack. General Adelbert Ames was to lead his infantry division through the Confederate minefield and rush the palisade at its' western end. Meanwhile a 2,000-man marine "boarding party" would simultaneous attack the eastern end of the palisade.

While the marine contingent suffered heavy losses, the infantry attack eventually succeeded in turning the Confederate flank by taking each bombproof in its turn. After a grim six-hour fight, in which the marine force lost 400 men, the Union flag flew over the landface of Ft. Fisher. Lamb's forces had no choice but to spike their guns and strike their colors. Union losses totaled 1,700 while Confederate losses totaled some 500.

There is a final tragic episode associated with this battle, however. Bivouacked in the area of, and even atop, the fort's main powder magazine were portions of three Union regiments. For reasons not fully agreed upon, a massive explosion of this magazine rocked the fort in the early morning hours of January 16. Some 200 men were killed, many in their sleep.

For the Confederate forces facing Sherman and Grant, if the end had not been clearly in sight before this battle, it was most certainly visible now. Charleston, South Carolina, was evacuated on February 18, 1865, and just four days later, on February 22, Union troops entered an abandoned Wilmington, North Carolina.

Letters from John D. Cottrell begin to dominate the collection. Frankly, his correspondence is often more insightful and illuminating anyhow as William's letters become more cynical and sarcastic. Maggie also kept her letters from other soldier friends such as Nick Hagerman, Charles Fenton, Joseph Brown, and John D. Fogarty. They have been included because of the color and continuity they add to the story and the collection.

Point Lookout, Maryland
January 7, 1865
Kind Friend Maggie,

   Although for the past four years this cruel war has separated our meetings, through all this long and lonely time, I have never forgotten that I have a friend. I must say that I have always cherished the thought of you, my friend. Would that I could only express my feelings in regards to a subject which I have already introduced. I can not and will not leave you in suspense. All I can say is this: enjoy yourself in any company you wish and go where you wish and with whom you will. It is all the same to me. Never think of my getting offended without reason. If you find anyone that you think will be more faithful and will suit you any better than your humble servant, you will not allow yourself to hesitate for a moment and change your mind.
   Please give me a long letter [to] tell me all the news and your opinion about what I have said in this letter and how it suits you.

                    Your True Friend
                    John D. Cottrell

Point Lookout, Maryland
Feb. 13, 1865
Good Evening Friend Mgr.,

   This pleasant Monday evening finds me still in the land of existence and able to improve a few leisure moments in penning you a short letter.
   Margaret, there has been no news yet, only of our late fight along the Southside Railroad and the total bought [by] the Rebels. The Rebel General H. Graham [was] killed. Our losses [are] estimated at

500 total killed, wounded and missing _____ estimated at 1250. Reports say that they will not reach that figure. But it is hard to say.

The weather is cold and stormy most of the time.

Bid you good bye,
John D. Cottrell

Letter not headed
February 22, 1865
Dear Friend Maggie,

It is snowing like fury, and I think this would be a good chance to write you a few lines. I have often thought about you and thought I would like to hear from you. You must excuse me for not writing to you before. It is a great consolation to the soldiers to hear from home.

Well, friend Maggie, I hardly know what to write to interest you. There isn't any news of any consequence. We have had a very bad weather and the mud is very bad. I heard that John H. Bord deserted on the 29th. They caught him, put him in the guard house and kept all his pay. I think that's too bad, don't you, Maggie? I imagine I can hear you say it is so. Well, he had no business to be a soldier, and another thing, he had no business to desert.

I remain your affectionate friend and well wisher,

Nick Hagerman
Co. D. 14th NJ Regt.
Frederick City, Maryland

Fort Powhaten
Army of the James
February 28, 1865
Friend Maggie,

I am not able to communicate anything of any interest to you at the present time as regards war matters. Everything is very quiet at this post at the present time. Also, there is very little cannonading in the front. They had a very sharp fight some two weeks ago on the left of the lines though none were engaged except the Fifth Corps. I believe [that] they gained some ground and still hold it.

There are a few [deserters] who come in here now and then. Some of our boys went out last Saturday and captured three. They tell the same old story about being starved out and naked and so on.[73]

We hear good news from Sherman. They say he is sweeping things in South Carolina like a tornado. I am in hope he may come up in the rear of Richmond. I think it will make the Rebs open their eyes.

The draft was postponed until the first of March. I think it will change if Sherman keeps going, although there [are] some in Jersey that I would like to see down here awhile. I think it would do them good, don't you?

They say it is very sickly up and around Jersey. They also say there are some whole families who have smallpox.

It not only kills a great number but leaves many disfigured. I am in hopes it does not get into the army.

Unsigned but possibly John D. Cottrell

Wilmington, North Carolina
March 1, 1865
Dear Sister,

We have our quarters in the city and the troops are fine. We have been here five days, but being out all the time this is the first time I have had an opportunity to write. There are only three teams in the brigade and it keeps a fellow a-jogging all the time. We are going to draw some more pay soon. The citizens in this town are pretty loyal thought thoroughly afraid. Last night the air was quiet all along the

---

[73] To encourage Confederate desertions, the Union command paid deserters $10 if they crossed over the lines with their weapons (Trudeau, 332).

lines. Our troops are encamped and there is not a Rebel within 10 miles of them. The city is about two or three times as big as Freehold.

The Rebels have been parading some 10,000 of our prisoners and it is an awful sight to see them. Some are naked and hardly able to walk the streets. The galoshes that Thomas sent me are in Paul Parkin's knapsack at Fort Fisher. He is taking care of them for me but I will be unable to get them for some time. All we lost this time was two wounded and none killed. Tell Thomas that Charles McCreaf is wounded.

William Jones

Point Lookout Maryland
March 9, 1865
Dear Friend Maggie,

For every day brings us new and good news. Now this morning's paper confirms the news of Sheridan's late move in the [Shenandoah] valley, his grand success and of capture of the Rebel General Early, his staff and 1700 of his command.[74] We heard of Sheridan's advance on the Lynchburg and Richmond Railroad. He will destroy it in spite of all the Rebels can do and then where will the army of General Lee look to get their supplies? J I think they will all come down with a rush and the old stars and stripes will soon find a place in the city of Richmond flying over the Rebel rags of treason and of insult to the country. The Rebels must give up soon and submit to the rules of Honest Abraham. In the morning papers I saw a short list of the guns that have been taken since December 15th and this

---

[74] The reference to the capture of Jubal Early was only a rumor. He fled the Shenandoah Valley after the March 2nd defeat at Waynesboro. Phil Sheridan and the Union Army thus controlled the valley. Early was relieved of command.

was only what was taken from Hood at Nashville, Tenn. by Gen. Thomas.[75]

General Sherman took Fort McAllister at Savannah. We hear of what was taken by General Gillmore at Charleston and the defenses of that place. And we hear that Generals Terry and Schofield, with the assistance of Admiral Porter's Naval Fleet, captured at Wilmington amounts to 800 men and 53 guns from the city's defenses and they are all in our hands. Besides the guns that they have blasted to pieces with their ironclads, they have destroyed Savannah, Charleston, and Wilmington. The loss of guns from the Rebels in this length of time will exceed 900. Compare this with our victories and look upon the dark side of our forlorn hope and then it will appear to look bright and more encouraging than it has for some time.

Now things appear to go very well and we will soon close this bloody strife.

I haven't heard any news from the regiment since last I wrote. I don't know where they are, but I suppose they have plenty to do down there and they don't get much time to write.

Well, my friend Margaret, it will soon be one year since you paid a visit to your friends at Fort Schuyler. This day finds me here on Point Lookout to spend the merry month of March. It is a place that looks more like a prison for convicts of the worst kind than a place to send Union soldiers. They have places for the Rebel spies and such. Old Harvey Brown thought that we were a hard crowd of chaps. He thought the best plan was to get us out of there as quickly as possible and we were not a bit sorry to get away from this prison. And now this is my prison. Yet this is not so bad, for there is some chance of escape from here. Now that the war looks pretty favorable, I think my chance is good to get out soon. And then, all the rest of

---

[75] According to official reports filed by Generals Hood and Thomas, Confederate losses in Hood's disastrous invasion of Tennessee ranged from 9,000 to 13,000.

the old boys that are left will return.

From your most affectionate friend,
Good-bye for this time.
Unsigned but probably John D. Cottrell

Camp Hooker, Maryland
March 16, 1865
Friend Maggie,

I received your kind letter. This afternoon I was very happy to hear that you are well. I am sorry to say that there have been 25 deaths in our regiment altogether, but none of your acquaintances. Maggie, we have had a great deal of dull, stormy weather here for quite sometime. It rains or snows almost regularly every other day. We had a bit of snow here yesterday. There are so many of us together that we never get lonesome. There is always something going on for pleasure and amusement. We have not seen many very hard times yet, but there are plenty of chances for hard times ahead of us. Maggie, there are rumors that we will go to the front as soon as the weather becomes more settled, but that is nothing more than we expect. We are ready any moment that we may be called upon. As for myself, I would like to have it [said] that I never harmed a fellow man, but if it is my duty, I shall do my duty as far as it lies in my power. Maggie, how many hearts it would make glad if this dreadful war would only come to a close, but then, alas, how many poor soldiers are there who will never return to their dear parents and friends who, like all others, left their homes with high hopes of returning. But so it must be, all cannot return. Maggie, please excuse me for writing such a tiresome letter but it is out the question for me to write any other kind.

Maggie, you spoke about the school room. It makes me think of old times [and of] the many happy hours I spent there. I was always such a blockhead that I never could learn.

Yours truly,
from well-wished friend,
Joseph Brown

Point Lookout, Maryland
March 16, 1865
Dear Friend M.E.J.,

This afternoon finds me in good health and spirits. Yet I hardly know how to address you on behalf of your brother for as yet I haven't received any letters from any one of my comrades concerning him. I had a letter from the regiment and they were at Wilmington. This friend said nothing of William. Yet, I believe that William is all right and as soon as he gets a chance to answer my letters I will hear from him. The weather has been very cold for some days past and today it is storming hard. If it doesn't stop soon there will be no mail to Point Lookout. Tonight and tomorrow will be another lonesome day with no news from any quarters. The latest news from the valley was of Sheridan's victory over the Rebel's army and the destruction of the Lynchburg and Richmond Railroad and of the Lehigh and Chesapeake Canal and how he put the Rebels to fight. The news is good from that quarter. Soon Sherman and Schofield's forces will combine and march through North Carolina.[76]

---

[76] Sherman was in overall command, but Schofield did play a significant role especially at the Battle of Bentonville. Fought on March 19-20, 1865, this fight has been called the "last stand in the Carolinas." With the defeat of Confederate forces there, the road to Goldsboro, North Carolina, and ultimately northward into Virginia was open. Sherman's drive through the Carolinas has been seen as one of the finest marches in military history as he overcame numerous terrain and climatic difficulties with extraordinary speed. His men drove 500 miles in eight weeks. Little of the Bentonville site has been preserved.

The Rebels are in great confusion.

From Your Affectionate Friend,
John D. Cottrell

Fort Powhatan
Army of the James
March 19, 1865
Friend Maggie,

This is a beautiful Sabbath afternoon, very pleasant and warm. I should like very much to be at home to enjoy it, however as I am permitted to be here I don't think I can put the day to any better use than penning a few lines to my loyal lady friend Maggie.

We are still in the same place and we think we shall spend the summer at this place although we cannot especially tell, for a soldier little knows how long he may stay in one place. We have a splendid regiment as we are in a place where we can keep ourselves clean. Our Colonel is also very strict with the men. They must keep clean or suffer the consequences. There are some who say they are tired of this place and want to go to the front. [Those who say this] have never been there.

We expect to hear important news from the front as it has been rumored for several days that Grant would attack the Rebels at the earliest hour. We also heard last evening that Sheridan would cross the James either last night or this morning between this place and City Point. All of the soldiers are saying that there won't be but one more fight. They also state that if Grant held his position three months longer he would have the greatest part of Lee's army without fighting as they are deserting in immense numbers every day and night.[77]

I suppose your brother has had very little chance to write if he is in Sherman's army since they have been on the move so much lately.

Yours,
Charles Fenton
Please reply soon!
Hammond General Hospital

Pensacola, Florida
March 19, 1865
Friend Maggie,

Last night I went to the theater; a sort of one that's sure dull going to, I can assure you. Every once and a while there is a spare Rebel comes to see us. They never care about going either. That's where the laughs come in. When I received your letter I just in the act of sitting down to dinner. My friend Will sings out, "Johnny, here is a love letter for you!" Well, I dropped the hash and took the letter and while I was reading, some gentleman's son took the last of my potatoes. You see they are a rare breed.

From your friend,
John D. Fogarty
U.S. Ship *Potomac*,
Pensacola Bay, Florida

---

[77] It has been estimated that Lee's once-proud Army of Northern Virginia was losing the equivalent of a regiment every two days due to the desertion stemming from demoralization and the realization that the "Lost Cause" was truly lost.

Point Lookout, Maryland
March 23, 1865
Friend,

This pleasant morning finds me yet in the land of the living and once more I will use the opportunity to pen you a short letter, the third of this week.

William is in good quarters in the city of Wilmington and of course will be all right there. He tells me that his health is very good and that he hasn't had any fighting since the taking of Wilmington. He and the boys of the company think that they can stay there for some time.

Friend Margaret, the opinion of all the leading men of the country think that the war is near to a close and that the Rebel General Lee has come out openly said that it useless for him to stand and fight without food, horses and reinforcements. [He said that] his army is completely over _____ and [that he] could not get them to fight anymore like they did in the many battles before. The diseases are numerous and they have gone to desertion in the open day light. They bring their arms and often their horses and mules into our lines. The present a hard appearance and tell hard stories of the situation in the Rebel army.

I shall close for the present,
John D. Cottrell

Point Lookout
April 2, 1865
Kind Friend Maggie,

Well, Maggie so long to a cold and stormy winter. And more, the armies of Grant, Sherman and Sheridan are still on the move and have so far been very successful. The news by telegraph a short time ago was this – the Rebel General Lee was anticipating an attack on their lines near Fort Stedman and had most of his fighters there. Instead, General Grant on Thursday morning last, the II and V army

Corps, with Sheridan's cavalry forces, moved to the left towards Hatcher's Run. The Rebels thought our lines had been somewhat weakened by the movements of those Corps so they made another bold and desperate attack on Fort Stedman. They were repulsed with heavy losses. The attack was made at 10 o'clock on Thursday night. After three desperate attempts to break our lines, yet they failed.[78] There were some prisoners taken – the number is not yet known – and on Friday the forces that composed the 2nd and 5th converged with Sheridan's cavalry at Hatcher's Run. On their way to the Southside RR after a short advance, they found the Rebel lines. There was only a short, brisk retreat of the Rebels to their lines of defense and there they made a stand. With a flanking movement our forces succeeded in capturing three entire brigades. The Rebels are shut in from all [sides] in their line of defenses south of Richmond and the news in a few days will be of great importance to our cause. About a hundred Rebels came here today after the latest capture and more of them are coming tonite.

The last news I have from the regiment was that they were going to _____. If I remember right, in a letter of a short time ago, you spoke of the awful news of so many brave and noble young fellows that will fall before the enemy. Our losses are comfortably small and the appearance of things at present looks as if there will soon be no more fighting. Sherman will annihilate Johnston's army and then there will only be the armies of Richmond to defend the capital of the Southern Confederacy.

Your true and affectionate friend,
John D. Cottrell

---

[78] A Rebel corps under General John B. Gordon made the Confederacy's last real offensive effort on March 25, 1865. Attacking at 4 A.M. His men succeeded in taking Fort Stedman and three nearby redoubts under the element of surprise, but by late morning of the same day Federal forces had counter-attacked and regained all positions lost. Gordon's force lost 2,000 captured and another 1,600 killed and wounded. The union forces could easily replace their 1,000-man loss; the Confederacy could not.

Pt. Lookout, Maryland
April 6, 1865
Kind Friend Maggie,

This morning finds me in remarkably good health and still on the Point in Maryland. I have no doubt but that you have heard of the fall of Petersburg and Richmond. The Rebel army is now on its retreat from their only strongholds now that the Rebel General Lee has been completely out-generaled by Grant. He has been forced to abandon his only hope and live at the mercy of the "murdering Yankees" as they say. The only thing he can think of is getting to join the Rebel J. Johnston and cut their way through Sherman's line to go further south. But the Army of [Northern] Virginia is almost surrounded. Grant is on their track and Sheridan is following them along the Southside Railroad [to] stop his crossing. General Hancock is in the valley and will check his advance further north; General Stoneman, with 40,000 cavalry and General Thomas with 25,000 infantry accompany him. [He] has started from Knoxville, Tennessee and is sweeping down through the valley of Virginia to join Sherman's forces in North Carolina. Kilpatrick's cavalry is raiding the North Carolina country and will soon communicate with Thomas and Stoneman. Then the Rebel armies will be completely cut in two and before either of those forces can be brought together, this force of ours will be a combined army and then the thought of peace and of the annihilation of the rebel armies will soon sound through the land.

[We have taken in] an immense quantity of guns and ammunition and about 18,000 Rebel prisoners. Within the last five days there has been 12,000 prisoners [who have] arrived here and still [more] appear to be coming. 900 arrived here this morning.

I have heard nothing more from William since I last informed you.

Yours Truly, J.D. Cottrell[79]

---

[79] There are errors based on faulty rumors in this letter, but it does not diminish the remarkable candor and sense of the "big picture" that Cottrell possessed.

Tharston's Station, North Carolina
April 9, 1865
Dear Brother,

I seat myself down to pen you a few lines to inform you that I am yet still here, gay and happy. Today is Sunday and tomorrow we move, where we will go I can't tell. Perhaps to cut Lee off from retreating too far south. This may be the last letter you will receive from me for sometime for if we are on the move I can't write. I can write but there are no mail leaves until we get to our destination. I am quite gay today because I have two canteens of whiskey on my wagon and it is just about as much as I can drink.

Now as I am just about half-full and two-thirds drunk, I will give you a word of advice – don't buy any stock more than you can get along with. If you can, clean the place and fix up the house. This would be much better than to buy a house and get us into more debt. Richmond is taken and I hope the war will soon be over, maybe in three more weeks.

Your affectionate brother,
William Jones

CHAPTER SIX

1865

Virginia and Home

This final segment of Maggie Jones' collection includes correspondence from William as well as quite a few letters from John D. Cottrell. In it we can see the soldiers' musings about postwar plans, their feelings about the death of President Lincoln, their participation in the Grand Review and their impatience over being released from service to return home as citizen soldiers. A surprise is contained in one of William's letters in August.

Point Lookout, Maryland
April 17, 1865
Kind Friend Maggie,

This is a very pleasant day. Everything looks like spring and the appearance of all seems to be glad of that glorious chance. Many of us feel that the sound of peace will soon crown all and the day will long be remembered by many of those who have felt the effects of this Civil War. I had a letter from William. He said the Rebels had all fled and there was nothing near them. There is a rumor here now that the Rebel General Johnston has surrendered to General Sherman. The truth is not yet known but we shall hear in a few days. Now if this report is not true, the news of a few days will decide the fate of Johnston's army, for General Sheridan and a heavier force have started for Weldon. They will completely annihilate the Rebel army under Johnston or compel him to surrender his force. The army of General Lee that was surrendered to General Grant is all being paroled and sent home. If they are caught in the army, they will be punished again very severely. The Rebels here are as glad over the war's end as if they had found a prize. A great part of the Rebel officers are here wanting to take the oath and get out of it.[80]

From your affectionate friend,
John D. Cottrell

Point Lookout, Maryland
April 24, 1865
Kind Friend Maggie,

The news from the army is good from all points. The surrender of the Rebel General Johnston is not yet confirmed. The rumors say that he has been taken. It may be true. I can not tell.

---

[80] Johnston's army surrendered to Sherman's forces at Durham Station, North Carolina on April 25th. This followed a week of negotiations over terms. Johnston and Sherman had first met on April 17, the date of the letter itself. As for the actual terms of surrender, Sherman almost certainly exceeded his authority in granting Johnston's army the right to return home not only with full pardons, but also with their property. By interpretation, this could even mean that they could retain their weapons and even their slaves back home. Furthermore, citizenship was restored and it was even suggested that the former Confederate states would be readmitted to the Union. This docu-ment was immediately rejected by President Andrew Johnson and Secretary of War Edwin Stanton. Hence, a new agreement had to be arranged between Sherman and Johnston, both of whom were pre-war and post-war friends. Sherman never forgot the rebuke and exacted a highly visible degree of public vengeance by ignoring Stanton on the reviewing stand on the day of the Grand Review. In addition, the "oath" referred to concerned an amnesty and allegiance oath required of all surrendering Confederate soldiery.

Maggie, you have heard of the murder of the President and all the particulars? To think of such a thing is enough, don't you agree? After all, I would not vote for him at the election but I am glad that he was re-elected and I am more glad to think he lived to know Richmond had been taken. He visited the Rebel City and sat on old Jeff's chair. Just as he was about to close the war, he has been cut down by the hand of a villain – a traitor who cried out after the fatal shot was fired that the South was revenged. For such an act there is no ground. I am sure that the man who has taken his place will show the South no such clemency. Their only hope is now blasted. Pardon will not be granted as free[ly] as it has been before. Andy Johnson has said that all offenders will be punished. Many of those Rebel officers who were on parole in Washington and around Richmond have been arrested and are now confined in Libby Prison. They are thought to know something of the conspiracy that was arranged to assassinate the president. Those engaged in willful murder must suffer the penalty of the law.

There is a 100,000 dollar reward for the body of Booth, the murderer, and as yet he has not been caught but his capture is certain.

John D. Cottrell

Point Lookout, Maryland
April, 1865
Kind Friend Maggie,

I think that I shall get home inside of six months. All of the soldiers wish the war to be crowned with glorious victory. My greatest wish has been to free myself of hospital life. I do not know how I shall make out. But I find I cannot get to my regiment and I have already applied for my discharge. If I succeed I shall be able to inform you at an earlier day, I hope. If I can get my discharge I will once more be a free man. You will please excuse my poor letter and bad writings for this is awful. Regards to you. I shall close hoping to hear from you.

From William

Partial letter not dated but probably April, 1865

You speak of the death of our beloved President. That was awful, I must confess. They have captured J. Wilk[es] Booth or rather got the satisfaction of knowing that he is no more. Another one of Booth's friends that accompanied him was taken alive. J.W. Booth was shot by a sergeant of the cavalry who was searching for him. They found him in a barn and requested him to surrender. He denied that and the villain was smoked out of his hiding place armed to the teeth. He showed no fight at all but declared surrender. But after all, he was made to surrender to the leaden missile of war from a cavalry sergeant's pistol and fell. His last words were to his mother. He said to tell her that he died for his country and he breathed his last farewell. The other one that was taken at the same time has confessed that he was assigned to murder Stanton. He said his hand failed him as the time of his appointment had come.[81] Now his fate lies in only a short space of time. His mind must be awfully troubled to think of his crimes. What had ought to be his share of punishment? Such punishment as he will get will be all together too good. The worst they could get for him would be too good for such an offense as to only think of attempting to cut down the head of the

---

[81] There was a larger-scale plot to assassinate key members of the government. Besides Booth's murder of the President, Lewis Powell was assigned to kill Secretary of State William Seward while George Atzerodt was to shoot Vice-President Andrew Johnson. Powell lost his nerve while Atzerodt attempted his assignment but failed to harm Seward as he tried in vain to slash and stab his intended victim. Seward, injured in a carriage accident just prior to the plot's execution, was saved by the heavy bandages which enshrouded him.

government. But they failed in their wicked plan and are caught at their own game and will swing without a doubt.

Now, I think that the country will be crowned with laurels while the South will be cast down and overwhelmed with grief and sorrow at their folly.

John Cottrell
Point Lookout, Maryland
20th Regt. V.R.C.

Ft. Powhaten
Army of the James
May 3, 1865
Friend Maggie,

Your long-looked-for-though-always-welcome-letter of the 21st came the last day of the month. I had almost come to the conclusions that you had forgotten your soldier friend, although better late than never.

We still remain in the same place but I am almost wild to get away from it. I never was in jail before, but just imagine yourself fastened within such a place as this for seven months and more. I can't compare it with anything nearer than being in jail. I suppose I ought not find fault but I am so sick of this place.

Things have been changed greatly in military affairs since I last wrote you. Everyone in this camp is rejoicing here on account of the recent victories of our armies. When the news of Johnston's surrender reached us there was a salute of 100 guns fired. The death of our president cast quite in gloom over the army and many a bitter curse was written against the assassin. I regret it very much myself, although I think we have a man who will fill his place in every respect, one whom I don't think will show them so many favors. I think they will find out that they have slain their best friend. They show great respect for the president in the army. Every flag is draped in mourning and nearly every soldier in the army wears crepe on his left arm. I am glad to think the assassin has met with what he so richly deserved. I hope all of his friends meet with the same.[82] If they do not they must get what they deserve. All the talk in this camp at present is about going home. I hope we may get home soon, as I think it will be very unhealthy here this summer. I am glad you have heard from your brother and you find him in good health. I hope he may continue so until his return home which I think will be soon, as I see in this evening's herald that the army is to be reduced by 400,000 and I think that will take nearly all the volunteers.

Unsigned but probably John D. Cottrell

Red Bank
May 6, 1865
Friend Maggie,

Your recent letter was received and _____ with pleasure. I have had no opportunity to write, only Sunday, as I have been very busy throughout the week since the death of President Lincoln.

The churches in Red Bank have been draped in mourning ever since and they look beautiful with the stars and stripes decorated with large rosettes of black and white cape.

---

[82] As John D. Cottrell noted in a previous letter, Booth was killed (according to official reports) in a barn fire on Garrett's Farm in Bowling Green, Virginia, on April 26. Atzerodt, Powell, David Herold, and boarding house matron Mary Suratt were hung on July 7, 1865. Four others were sentenced to prison. While one of the conspirators died in Fort Jefferson prison in Florida, three others were eventually pardoned by President Johnson in 1869. Mary Surrat, Dr. Samuel Mudd and Ford's Theatre stagehand Edman Spangler probably were all innocent of the charges levied. Mudd's name was ultimately cleared by his descendants. His "crime" had been that of setting and treating Booth's leg which had been broken during the assassination. Some doubt was raised in 1992 about whether or not it was John Wilkes Booth who had died in the aforementioned barn fire.

I received a letter from my old friend J.D.C. the same evening I received yours. It was from Point Lookout, dated April 29th. He was well when he wrote, but his mind was so unsettled with the good news of the rebellion being over that he could not write a long letter.

Well, I would like to know when the veterans get discharged. I would like to be around as I think there would be a good time.

With respect and good wishes to you and the family in general.

I remain respectfully yours,
John A. Woodside
In care of Sidney McBlume
Camp Hooker, Monocacy Bridge, Maryland

Raleigh, North Carolina
May 7, 1865
Sabbath Afternoon
Dear Sister,

Your kind and affectionate letter of the 16th of April arrived this morning. We are stationed here at this place as the war is played out. There will be no more marching. Had I taken what was offered me the other day, I would have been on my way home now. I was offered a sergeancy and 30 days furlough to reenlist. To go home now is my wish. To go home in two or thee months would be spending money for nothing. And to go back in the company, this would not do even if they should cover me all over with stripes. Francis A. Fielder has gone home on furlough.

The devil couldn't persuade me to go home for 30 days even with three stripes on my arms. I will close still remaining your affectionate brother.

William Jones

Hope to be home inside of five months sooner or later. Good bye. Those two boys that the war took are back all right; got robbed of their clothes and money but made their escape. Well, this cruel war's over and we kicked the _____ the Confederacy.

> To My Friends at Home
> *An undated refrain*
> Dear Friends, how oft I think of thee,
> And the joys of days gone by.
> When I took thy gentle hand, Maggie,
> And said a last "Good Bye."
> Those days were buds of blooming youth,
> Perchance we'll see again.
> But months have passed, yea that happy thought
> Of meeting thee again.
> And when the papers you read o'er,
> And see the list of slain,
> Thousands fell to rise no more
> While thousands moan with pain.
> Perchance my name you'll notice there,
> If in battle slain should be.
> One boon[?] I ask of thee that's near,
> Then Maggie think of me.
>   -J.D.C.

Camp Hoffman,
Point Lookout, Maryland
May 14, 1865
Dear Friend

This friend of mine, Mr. Thompson, who you saw at Fort Schuyler, thinks we will soon get home. If I am not much mistaken we will be coming with all the other veterans here, too. But they are so few now after such a fall of hard fighting. To think of the many veterans that were at home in the month of February 1864 and now to look at the number that are left, no one can imagine the number we have lost. Also, we have lost many others who were not veterans and now the awful temptation for some – they are offering _____ to go to Mexico to clear the French out of there.[83] There are many who will go at the first chance. The sight of the country would be worth something. The will not find the valleys of Virginia to march through but rather a sandy desert and not a spring of water near them. Some may think they will have good times there but they will be fooled if such is their opinion. Now that the war is closed, let the government discharge the volunteers and enlist regulars. The can put all they want there in a little while if they only discharge the volunteers. Now my sheet is nearly full. I hope my soldiering is nearly done. If so, there will be noting to write at all, only to look over the papers and find out what the French are doing in Mexico.

From your affectionate friend,
John D. Cottrell

---

[83] France, Spain, and England attempted to test the waters of the western hemisphere by sending troops to Mexico in 1861. Their belief in the preoccupation of the United States with its Civil War emboldened them to this plan. France made the most concerted effort and by the spring of 1862, French Emperor Napoleon III had placed his nephew Maximilian on the vacant Mexican seat of power. Spain and Britain thus withdrew their interest. Confronted with insidious guerilla warfare for four years, Maximilian tried to carry on the pretense of rule. Later abandoned by his own country and facing a 50,000-man force being mobilized by General Philip Sheridan, Maximilian was isolated. Captured on May 14, 1867, he was tried and subsequently executed on June 19, 1867. He and his wife Carlotta remain as historically tragic figures caught up in events and circumstances beyond any European control.

Also caught up were some 3,000 expatriot Confederate exiles who fled the re-united United States. They were led by Generals Edwin Kirby-Smith and Jo Shelby. Virtually all of them, when the dust settled from the Maximilian affair, lost their land holdings, fortunes, and even their lives.

Camp Cadwalader, Philadelphia
June 13, 1865
Dear Friend Maggie,

Discharges from the army are still coming. Here from the field they will all be mustered out of the army and sent to the Grand Review.[84] Last Saturday it was formed close to our camp and had looked very well. They would have made a very handsome sight had it not been for the dreadful rain shower that came down. It started as the line of men came up and it kept up till the review was all over. The line was formed on Columbia Avenue and [went] the distance of two miles down Broad Street. We then crossed town to Front Street. They had a splendid dinner at the Union Volunteer Relief Saloon. Troops went all over the city, some to their homes and others to their camps.

From your friend
John D. Cottrell
Co. F, 20th Regt., VRC

Raleigh, North Carolina
June 28, 1865
Dear Brother,

After a long silence I seat myself down to pen you a few lines and inform you I still exist.

I don't like the southern states as farming country although they do raise fine crops of corn and sweet potatoes; round potatoes do not grow very large. The manure is scarce. Cotton is raised in all parts and wheat is productive in some parts. They plant their corn in the rain.

---

[84] Veterans of the Union Army returned home to tumultuous crowds in cities like Philadelphia. The Grand Review held in Washington, D.C., on May 23-24, 1865 paraded 200,000 soldiers up Pennsylvania Avenue.

People who were rich before the ware are now as poor as turkeys and have to pick berries and plums and all sorts of things to make a living.

For the future, the poor mans' chance is the best. In the past there had been no public schools but there will be in the future.

The negroes are almost starving to death. Their former masters had to let them go. Some find work; some none.

Still remaining your affectionate Brother,
William Jones

Raleigh, North Carolina
June 30, 1865
Dear Sister Maggie,

Received a letter from J.D. today. I am going to enjoy the pleasures of peace just as well as the hardships of war. As I close my eyes to slumber at night, I think of the gay comrades that drape my side in the open-field fights of last summer's campaign. Some lay on the field; others are buried by the dim twinkle of the stars. Poor George R. The night he left the main line, he rose to go to the picket line. "George, be careful. Do not be too reckless in the future." "I will, Bill," came the answer. The next morning at eight o'clock, he was laid low. That evening we buried him under an oak tree along side of John H. Graham who was killed the day before trying to get my breakfast to me. I was detached from the rest of the pickets. A sharpshooter could get them so we had to crawl as the Rebels were only a 190 yards away from our [lines]. He tried to get me coffee at sunrise but got shot through the heart. When the cooks returned to the works they told Lt. Tantum. They found but me and said they could not get to me. I would not look for anyone to cross that open field in broad daylight, so close to the Rebel marks as that and with no trees to shade him.

The first three years, he and I could seldom agree, but the latter part of his time he could seldom do enough for me.

William

Camp Cadwalader
Philadelphia
July 3, 1865
Dear Friend Maggie,

I find in the papers that they are discharging the old veterans and if such is true, the 48th will soon be coming home. Then I shall get my papers. They have been sent to all of the old veterans of '61'. A good many of the New York regiments have been sent home for the past week and perhaps before another week is over, I may soon be returning with the rest. I am entitled to my discharge under the recent orders from the War Department.

I had a letter from William sent to me some time ago but if you hear of William coming home, please tell me in your next letter.

From your most affectionate friend,
John D. Cottrell

Quartermasters Department
Raleigh, North Carolina
Aug. 6, 1865
My Dear Sister Maggie,

A few days ago I wrote home telling them I would write no more for I expected to soon be home. This is a cause for my tone to be changed. The corps is to be broken up or is already. One brigade is to be reorganized out of this whole corps and sent to Texas.

Whether our regiment is the one to go I can not tell, but I hope not. What troops stay in Raleigh will be here until January. Still this is not the cause of my dropping confidence. There is eight months pay due to us and no sign of any pay. In regards to the ladies, I am doing very well. I have been engaged to be married. Since I came home [I] slipped the cable each time and I have put off my wedding until Christmas. I think [that] I will be home by that time. I could marry some old widow down here [who might be] pretty well off if it were not for the snuff stuck in her mouth. I am slightly acquainted with an old widow who owns a fine house. I told her yesterday I wanted to get married but I wanted one about 45 years of age. She might pass for that if she had her teeth filed. Please excuse my criticizing for I know if you know her you would do the same. Today I find her trusting and flirting around. I promise to see her this evening. I will now close still remaining, your affectionate brother.

William Jones[85]

Annapolis, Maryland
August 8, 1865
Dear Sister,

We heard they were going to transfer some of our company. This is good. There are 26 of us out in the town. This city is under martial law. We don't go into camp except for our meals. We stay in a ballroom. It used to be drill room for the Department. There are enough swords to supply a regiment. We have fine times here sitting around. We pick on every soldier that we meet without a pass; some of them are drunk and abusive. We expect to leave here soon. We are here with the 26th New Hampshire. They're northers and they're just the best fellows that I have ever come across in my travels. We take turns, one gang goes out at a time, so it is not very hard for us. We met some of the Washington Grays and the 47th New York Regiment. They had a sergeant with them and he seems to be very big. On Monday night, he was patrolling along the street and he stopped at a hotel about 12 o'clock. He made them give him two quarts of whiskey. He gave them a forged note from the colonel. The man did not want to let him have it. The sergeant said that he didn't care a damn for no man. He was going to have what he wanted for

---

[85] The intended bride of William Jones was named Hattie. William eventually had five children: Francis (b. 1867), Jessie (b. 1868), Agnes (b. 1870), Ira (b. 1873), and William, Jr. (b. 1875).

this city was under martial law. That night the colonel took charge and put this young sergeant in the guard house. I may close my notes now as I am scant of paper. The names of the boys who transferred were Alexander Hires, David Brassel, Henry Atnens and Jon Gurke. They were crying like children when we got to camp.

Affectionate brother 'til death,
W.J.

Brooklyn
November 1865
Dear Sister Maggie and all the rest,

I seat myself this rainy Sabbath with my pen in hand to write to you after this long silence. I received a letter from Thomas on Thursday as he was going home on Wednesday. Johnston was very ill.

I mean to take care of a little baby for a lady who was going to East New York with her husband who is a captain of a company of horse soldiers. As for Thomas, I was not aware he was home yet or I would have sent him papers. I wrote twice to the company each time sending letters for the boys. I received replies from William and John A. Woodside. As for Woodside, I did not even think he was home yet. Tell him the 48th is here in Brooklyn now. I have not heard from William in four or five weeks.

Your sister Janie

Hoboken, New Jersey
September 22, 1865[86]
My Dearest Maggie,

My blood chills, for you know how we once parted. I think of the last hour when I allowed my angry passions to deceive me to induce me to the belief that I only fancied you, not loving you. But the bitterness of the succeeding day[s] more than punished me for my folly. Now I solemnly affirm that the love kindled in my breast shall never die out, but [will] grow into a widespread flame that shall illuminate both our souls. I will confidently assert that my whole affections are centered upon the first love of my youth. Maggie, if after reading this you cannot appreciate [it], burn it. I cannot bear sneers. But if you will remain true to me I will bind myself in ties which are endurable for without you, [my] life would seem a blank.

Well, Maggie, I must give you an imaginary kiss and say good night. Think of what I have said.

Calvin Havens

---

[86] This letter is included purely for the sentimentality it expressed. Furthermore, it is placed slightly out of chronological context because it seems a fitting endnote to this collection of letters.

CONCLUSION

In concluding this collection of letters, it is appropriate to finish with an excerpt from Palmer's regimental history of the 48th New York State Volunteers.

And now that we have come to the end of this history, and look back at the four long years through which it has been traced thus imperfectly, shall we not all feel proud of the noble part our dear old regiment bore! It has made the poor chronicler of its deeds love it more than ever. What battles it fought, what marches it made, what sufferings it endured for the Republic! Its career has been traced for you, comrades (and for your children), amid many difficulties, all the way from its organization at Fort Hamilton in the summer of 1861, to Washington and Annapolis, in the expedition to Port Royal Ferry, on Dausfuskie (sic), building the batteries on the mud islands on the Savannah River, in Fort Pulaski, and on Tybee; at Coosawhatchie and Bluffton (sic), to St. Helena and Folly Islands, at the storming of Morris Island, at the assault of Fort Wagner, at Olustee; then in the Army of the James at Chester Heights, Drewry's Bluff, Cold Harbor, Petersburg mine explosion, Deep Bottom, Strawberry Plains, Capin's Farm, New Market Heights, Fort Gilmer, Fort Fisher, Wilmington, Raleigh, and back to New York again. It went to the field in 1861 with 964 men; and during the four years about 1250 recruits and transfers were added to it. Its losses in battle were nine hundred and forty-seven, and one hundred and twenty-seven deaths from disease. Let us not claim for it honors superior to those of many other regiments in the army; but its career lasted through the whole four years, and whatever work was assigned to it, that it did faithfully.[87]

---

[87] Palmer, *The History of the Forty-Eighth New York State Volunteers,* 194.

AFTERWORD

140 Years Later...

One of the most interesting aspects of the research for this book involved actual visitation to the sites referred to in the letters. While time and travel constraints did not allow me to visit every site, those at Petersburg, Virginia; Fort Fisher, North Carolina; and Charleston, South Carolina proved very enlightening.

The most viable sites are Fort Pulaski, Georgia, and the Petersburg Battlefield. They are both in remarkable states of preservation although, due to the far-reaching nature of the campaign, segments of the latter have been lost to private development. Despite this, breastwork, abbatis, cannon batteries, and even The Crater are still there. Both sites are listed in the National Registry of Historic Sites and both are managed by the National Park Service. So is Drewry's Bluff, south of Richmond and the site of John D. Cottrell's wounding. The earthen fort complex remains in good preservation atop its impressively commanding view of the James River.

Charleston, South Carolina, is simply a beautiful city. For the historian, visits to Forts Sumter and Moultrie beckon. While they are both in excellent preservation, the latter is accessible by car on to Sullivan's island and the former by tour boat alone. At the southern side of the harbor channel is Morris Island. On it were Batteries Gregg at Cummings Point and Wagner at the narrow neck of the island. Neither fort remains. Morris Island is inaccessible except by boat and according to tour guides at Ft. Sumter, the remains of Ft. Wagner have long since eroded into the Atlantic Ocean. Morris Island is a barrier island and a certain transience comes with the turf. (Note the interchangeable usage of Ft. Wagner and Battery Wagner. This is acceptable in that Confederate sources generally refer to the fortifications as "Battery _____" while Federal sources call prefer the term "Fort _____.")

Folly Island, Hilton Head Island, and Daufuskie Island have all experienced varying degrees of commercial and private development. Union fortifications on Hilton Head Island, built to secure the area as a base of operations, exist in the remains of Fort Mitchel. Fort Fisher, not to be confused with an earthwork near the western end of the Union lines at Petersburg, remains near the mouth of the Cape Fear River in North Carolina. Much of the seaward rampart of the work, which was originally a mile-long fortification of mounded earth, logs and batteries, also has eroded into the sea. However, enough of the landward side is still there for the visitor to get a strong sense of the fort's impressive ramparts, bombproofs, and wooden palisade.

At each of the viable sites, including Ft. Fisher, there is a Visitor's Center that is indeed worth a look. If one is as passionate about the Civil War as this visitor is, he or she sees more, with the mind's eye, than mere ramparts and cannon...

Editorial remarks

The discovery, translation, and editing of these letters has truly been a fascinating assignment, as it would be for any teacher and student of the Civil War.

Among the impressions which struck me most has been the lack of military censorship. There are only a few references to any such thing in the letters and certainly by today's standards, one has to be impressed by the candor with which the letters are written. Names of regiments, duty stations, military operational plans and even dates of proposed movements are all explicitly written out. Reflecting on the degree of censorship which was prevalent during the recent Gulf War, the reader of these letters can appreciate the openness and at the same time, wonder how such candor was allowed. Moreover, the value letters such as these may have held had they fallen into enemy hands is interesting to contemplate.

A second afterthought lies in the sheer volume of letters that the brothers and their friends wrote. It seemed that they were always harping on poor Maggie to write more often. While data on the number of war letters emanating from Union soldiers stationed with the Jones brothers along the Carolina coast or from the Army of the James is lacking, perhaps this note, taken from an edition of the New York Times dated January 24, 1864 may shed some light. The source quoted Nashville, Tennessee's army post office and it said that 50,000 to 60,000 letters arrived daily and "the number reached 70,000 on several occasions." This figure is eye opening when one considers that the Union armies generally ranged in size from 60,000 to 120,000. It bespeaks of not only a high literacy rate, but also of the loneliness of soldiers anxious for news from home and conscious of the fact that they were engaged in making history.

It is hoped that these letters shed some modest light on the lives of ordinary soldiers in the Civil War and bring them and their adventures to life. They all shared, as Oliver Wendell Holmes, himself a veteran, noted, "...the incommunicable experience of war." These young men, whose words we have just read, did indeed communicate their experience and they did so in quaintly eloquent terms.

Inevitably, errors may have been made in translation and editing but they are hopefully minimal and inconsequential. The responsibility, however, rests totally with the editor with apologies to the reader.

A Word on Transcription

Handwritten letters from any era are always difficult to translate and transcribe. After photocopying the original letter, students in my classes at Brookdale Community College and Manasquan High School (the latter being U.S. History I Honor students), were given copies of *The Handwriting of American Records of a Period of 300 Years,* by E. Kay Kirkham (Everton Press, Logan, Utah) to help identify script patterns. The students were asked to correct misspelled words in their translations but were asked to leave the syntax in its original form. Some editing of the syntax was done by myself in order to make the letters read more smoothly and to clarify certain meanings. The original wording was left intact whenever possible. Punctuation was added. Further "cleaning up" was done by the typists, Diana Griggs-Fummey and Laura Butkus, but the integrity of the original wording was honored.

Most of the letters were originally written in ink, hence their preservation was remarkable. Those letters written in pencil are essentially lost to translation, but they comprise no more than about 7% of the collection. Gaps in the letters, as you read them, signify words which were utterly unreadable and indecipherable.

SELECTED BIBLIOGRAPHY

The American Civil War is the most written-about event in American History. The reader of these letters who seeks a deeper understanding of the events referred to may wish to read these works.

Bilby, Joseph, *The Irish Brigade*, Conshohoken, PA: Longstreet House, 1997.

Bishop, Jim, *The Day Lincoln Was Shot*, New York: Harper, 1955.

Burton, E. Milby, *The Siege of Charleston, 1861-1865*, Columbia, SC: University of South Carolina Press, 1970.

Chaitin, Peter, *The Coastal War: Chesapeake Bay to Rio Grande*, Alexandria, VA: Time-Life Books, 1984.

Dupuy, R. Ernest and Dupy, Trevor N., *The Encyclopedia of Military History*, New York: Harper and Row Publishers, 1970.

Foote, Shelby, *The Civil War: A Narrative History*, v. 2, New York: Random House, 1963.

Faster, Stephen, *The Civil War: A Narrative History*, v. 3, New York: Random House, 1974.

Gerraty, John A., *Historical Viewpoints*, v. 1, New York: Harper Collins, 1991, 6th edition.

Gillmore, Quincy A., *Siege and Reduction of Fort Pulaski*, Gettysburg, PA: Thomas Publications, 1988.

Gragg, Rod, *Confederate Goliath, The Battle of Fort Fisher*, New York: Weiner Publications, 1991.

Julian, Allen P, "The Siege of Fort Pulaski" reprinted in *Fort Pulaski and the Defense of Savannah*, Eastern Acorn Press, 1970.

Kennedy, Frances H., ed., *The Civil War Battlefield Guide*, Boston: Houghton Mifflin, 1990.

Lattimore, Ralston B., *Fort Pulaski*, Washington, D.C.: National Park Service Handbook #18, U.S. Government Printing Office, 1961.

McPherson, James, *Ordeal By Fire*, v. 2: *The Civil War*, New York: McGraw Hill Publishing, 1993, 2nd edition.

_____. *Battle Cry of Freedom*. New York: Oxford University Press, 1988.

National Park Service, *Fort Sumter, Anvil of War*, Washington, D.C.: U.S. Government Printing Office, 1984.

Palmer, Abraham J., *The History of the Forty-Eighth New York State Volunteers in the War for the Union*, New York: Charles Dilligham, 1885.

Pfanz, Harry W., *Gettysburg – The Second Day*, Chapel Hill, NC: University of North Carolina Press, 1987.

Rolle, Andrew, *The Lost Cause*, Norman, OK: University of Oklahoma Press, 1965.

Robertson, James, *Tenting Tonight*, Alexandria, VA: Time-Life Books, 1984.

Stevens, Joseph E. *1863: The Rebirth of a Nation*. New York: Bantam Books, 1999.

Taylor, Susie King, *A Black Woman's Civil War Memoirs*, New York: Weiner Publications, 1991.

Trudeau, Noah Andre, *The Last Citadel*, Boston: Little, Brown, & Company, 1991.

Wiley, Bell I., *The Life of Billy Yank: The Common Soldier of the Union*, Baton Rouge: Louisiana State University Press, 1983.

INDEX

Published by Mercer University Press
June 2000

Book design by Marc A. Jolley.
Jacket Design by Jim Burt.
Photograph on jacket: The 48th New York at Fort Pulaski.
Text font: Book Antiqua.
Printed and bound by Sheridan Books, Chelsea, Michigan.
Cased and covered with cloth, smyth-sewn, and printed on
    acid-free paper.